Toward a Theology of Evangelism

The Julian Hartt Library
Series Editor
Jonathan R. Wilson

****

Toward a Theology of Evangelism
Being Known and Being Revealed
The Lost Image of Man
Theology and the Church in the University
A Christian Critique of American Culture
The Restless Quest
Theological Method and Imagination
What We Make of the World: Memoirs of Julian Hartt

Toward a Theology of Evangelism

JULIAN N. HARTT

Wipf & Stock
PUBLISHERS
Eugene, Oregon

Wipf and Stock Publishers
199 W 8th Ave, Suite 3
Eugene, OR 97401

Toward a Theology of Evangelism
By Hartt, Julian and Hauerwas, Stanley
Copyright©1955 by Hartt, Julian
ISBN 13: 978-1-59752-780-4
Publication date 8/3/2006
Previously published by Abingdon Press, 1955

Scripture quotations are from the Revised Standard Version of the Bible and are copyright 1946 and 1952 by the Division of Christian Education of the National Council of the Churches of Christ in the U. S. A.

To
N. B. H.

Series Foreword

Why is Wipf and Stock reprinting the works of Julian Hartt? Certainly his faculty appointments and administrative responsibilities at Yale (1943-1972) and Virginia (1972-1981), after an initial term at Berea, indicate something of his participation in a formative period for American theological education. That observation, however, does not identify the impact of his work or the reasons for reprinting his books. His work deserves reprinting and renewed attention for at least four reasons.

One reason for reprinting Hartt's work is the depth of theological reflection represented in it. The books are not easy to enter. They are densely packed and cannot be read quickly. My first encounter with his work occurred in the basement of the library at the University of British Columbia. I was browsing in the religion section and was drawn to a book by its aesthetic appeal. Its size and proportions as well as its dusty blue color drew me in. I could not read the title on its spine, so I took it off the shelf: *A Christian Critique of American Culture*. Intrigued, I borrowed it from the library and renewed the loan several times while I managed to read about one-third of the book. I finally returned the book to the library and did not read it again until many years later.

So, let's be clear. Hartt's work makes significant demands on readers. His own erudition and his ability to bring it together in concentrated form means that his work cannot be skimmed for the "high points." Every book is packed with high points. Each paragraph makes an important contribution to the argument or exposition. Hartt's books, then, are not quick and easy reads. But such characteristics also mean that reading carefully through one of Hartt's books teaches more than sprinting through numerous other works. In an age that values short paragraphs, shallow thinking, and predigested ideas (that is, pablum), Hartt's books are strong meat not thin gruel.

Our age needs the kind of work that makes us slow down, chew on a sentence, a paragraph, an argument, until it has nourished our lives. That's what Hartt's work provides for us.

A second reason for making Hartt's work more readily available is not just its character but also its content. Hartt's work is not only densely packed, it is also sharply penetrating. One of Hartt's friends told me about once hearing him preach in a British Methodist church on Good Friday. "I felt like I had been laid bare, stripped of every pretense, lacerated by the truth, so that I could be healed by the gospel."

In Hartt's work, readers will find a severe truth-telling grounded in the conviction that only the truth revealed in Christ will set us free. So Hartt's penetrating insight and prophetic truth strips away our platitudes and the thin lies that we wrap around ourselves to protect us from the admission that our emptiness and anxiety go to our very core. Even though—perhaps precisely because—Hartt exposes these lies in their particular cultural expressions, his severity continues to administer healing grace to us today. Our particular cultural expressions of the lies and illusions that we create for ourselves may differ, but our propensity to live by lies and illusions remains a part of every human condition.

We must go one step further to understand why the content of Hartt's work is so penetrating. Its power lies not only in his clear-eyed perception of the lies we live by; even more, the power of his work lies in his apprehension of the gospel of Jesus Christ. My use of the word *apprehension* here is very important. Hartt has been apprehended by the gospel, and in the outworking of that gospel in his life, he has also apprehended it. This notion of apprehension is crucial to Hartt's thinking. Though he had this understanding of apprehension early in his intellectual development, it is highly developed in the work of Austin Farrer, who contributed significantly to Hartt's thinking. Today, a similar notion may be found in Reinhard Hütter's notion (in *Suffering Divine Things*) of being "rapt" by God.

For Hartt, to be apprehended by the gospel is to be so captured by God's grace in Jesus Christ that all things are seen by its light. All of our "unreality systems" are exposed as antihuman distortions of the way to human flourishing. So the gospel of Jesus Christ discloses the Rule of God in which we truly find the flourishing of all creation. Without this conviction, Hartt's brilliant exposure of our lies plunges us into despair. But in the light of the good news that Jesus Christ has overcome all that we fear, all that we deny, all our anxieties, all Sin, we are now free to confess the truth of our sin because the grace of God is greater still.

This double-edged truth makes Hartt's theology an invaluable witness to our age. We seem to combine cynicism about intentions in the exercise of human powers with a fatalism about the inevitability of misguided optimism that "this one time" we will achieve our intentions, which, when achieved, turn out not to be our salvation but our continuing damnation—and that by our own hands. In the midst of such darkness and despairing, the light and hope of Christ announce God's salvation for a damned humanity.

Hartt's perceptive and profound witness to this good news illuminates our world, penetrates the armor of lies, breaks the chains of sin, and sets us free to follow Christ. For these reasons, his work equips us for the mission to which the Lord and Savior of the church has called us.

A third reason for reprinting and reading Hartt's work is his impact on North American theology. Although Hartt is not well-known, during his twenty-nine years at Yale and ten years at Virginia he exercised enormous influence on a whole generation of theologians. Hartt himself had relatively few doctoral students. Many suggest that his high standards and fierce rhetoric put many students off. Hartt was a skilled debater who appears to have seldom adjusted his style according to circumstance. During Hartt's years at Yale, the school produced a majority of North America's theologians for a generation. Many of these theologians have acknowledged to me in private correspondence that Hartt's influence upon them is strong even if they do not consider themselves to be one of Hartt's students. (There is also the untold and controversial role that Hartt played in a struggle over control of the graduate program in religion.)

But there are also many who trained or taught at Yale and Virginia who have publicly acknowledged Hartt's impact: Diogenes Allen, Stephen Crites, James Gustafson, David Bailey Harned, Ray Hart, Van Harvey, Stanley Hauerwas, Gordon Kaufman, Walter Lowe, and John Sykes. Anyone who knows the work of these men (and most of the graduates in those days were men; one notable exception is Sallie McFague who was a student of H. Richard Niebuhr but who also served as teaching assistant to Hartt) will be intrigued by Hartt's role in their work. Two of Hartt's greatest fans are James Gustafson and Stanley Hauerwas, whose theologies have developed along quite divergent paths. For Hartt to be acknowledged by such influential and wildly diverse thinkers means that his work deserves careful attention.

Moreover, Hartt's work has received attention from contemporary Anabaptist and Baptist theologians. John Howard Yoder references Hartt's work briefly and appreciatively. James Wm. McLendon, Jr., gives Hartt sustained attention in developing the last volume of his "baptist" theology, *Systematic Theology, Volume 3: Witness*.

Does this diversity mean that Hartt is hopelessly incoherent or so obscure that he can be taken to mean anything? Not at all. Rather, this diversity means that Hartt's thought is rich in depth and generous in its embrace. Hartt seemed to many of his peers to have read and assimilated everything, or almost everything, of importance to the work of theology. At the same time, he did not lose his creative powers. Thus, through the assimilative and creative power of his intellect he produces seminal work that contains the seeds of many fruitful theological endeavors.

Finally, we need Hartt's work available to us today because he wrote as a theologian for "America." Hartt grew up on the American prairies with Hubert Humphrey as his childhood friend. Like many he returned often to those wide-open skies that represented for him the possibilities of American culture. But given his clear-eyed perception of our lies and illusions and his apprehension of the truth of Jesus Christ, he also saw the cultural embodiment of anxiety that distorts and corrupts the flourishing of life in the human creation that we call America. Today, in the midst of the rise of "the American Empire," Hartt's prophetic and subtle analyses are more desperately needed than ever.

So, for these four reasons, at least, we need Hartt's witness to the gospel of Jesus Christ in our midst. In the seven volumes that make up "The Julian Hartt Library," a new generation of readers will have available to them the major works of this seminal "American" theologian. I have written the Introduction to this present volume. I wrote above about my first encounter with Hartt's work. I had set it aside by the time I arrived at Duke for graduate studies in 1986. In the course of preparing to write a dissertation on Austin Farrer under the guidance of Tom Langford, I discovered that Hartt had used Farrer's work in his classes at Yale. One evening, prior to the start of Stanley Hauerwas's Theological Ethics Seminar, I asked him if he thought that Hartt would be open to a visit from me to talk about Farrer's work. "Sure," he said. "But you know you should think about writing on Julian. No one has taken a close look at him." With Tom Langford's encouragement, that's what I did. Writing on Hartt and continuing to draw on his work for my own vocation has been a wonderful adventure. I am grateful to Julian Hartt for the work he has done, to Stanley Hauerwas for his insight, to Tom Langford for his guidance, and to Wipf and Stock for their impetus to republish these works.

Jonathan R. Wilson
Acadia Divinity College, 2005

Foreword

Toward a Theology of Evangelism is written by a theologian. For most people—that is, people innocent of the character of theology in modernity—that *Toward a Theology of Evangelism* was written by a theologian would not seem strange. But for some time those concerned about evangelism, as well as those writing about it, have not been theologians. They have been sociologists or people that specialize in marketing, which makes it all the more important that Julian Hartt's *Toward a Theology of Evangelism* is to reappear. If the church is to recover a proper sense of evangelism, that is, an understanding of evangelism that is not equated with church growth, Hartt's wonderful book will be a crucial resource.

I have no idea what led Professor Hartt to write *Toward a Theology of Evangelism*, but I wish I knew the background story. Even in 1955, before theology had become desperate to separate itself from the church, a theologian would not naturally write a book on evangelism. Evangelism just did not seem to be an intellectually interesting theological topic. H. Richard Niebuhr's *Christ and Culture* and the first volume of Paul Tillich's *Systematic Theology* were published in 1951. I suspect if you asked most people in American theology from 1950 to 1955 they would have associated "real" theology with Niebuhr and Tillich. What kind of theologian would write on evangelism?

The answer, of course, is that a theologian as unique as Julian Hartt would write on evangelism. Julian, son of a Methodist minister in South Dakota, was not about to be intimidated by what might be considered "real" theology by the establishment. Julian, moreover, was able to write on evangelism because he was from a long line of Methodist ministers from New England. He had inherited with the drinking water in the parsonage the assumption that evangelism is not one thing among others the church may do. Evangelism is the heart of the church.

I do wonder, however, if Julian was asked to write this book by some agency of the Methodist Church. *Toward a Theology of Evangelism* was published by Abingdon Press. This was the only book Julian published with Abingdon, which at least suggests he may have been asked to write the book by a Methodist. I suspect if such was the case those who had asked him to write on evangelism may well have been disappointed, for what they got was a small systematic theology in which Julian presented most of the themes he would later develop over his long and fruitful career. Anyone desiring a short introduction to Hartt's theology can do no better than *Toward a Theology of Evangelism*. Indeed I would recommend that before anyone reads *A Christian Critique of American Culture* they read *Toward a Theology of Evangelism* because in this book Hartt provides an overview of the major themes of *A Christian Critique of American Culture*.

Hartt's book on evangelism was bound not to find a readership. I have no idea how many copies of the book were sold, but I suspect that it was not a best seller. Academic theologians would have ignored a book on evangelism as not really what theology should be about. Ministers, who at that time still thought it important to read theology, might have found the book far too "intellectually demanding." Hartt's work often failed to find the audience it deserved because he was doing serious theology in a manner that defied the easy distinction between systematic and practical theology. For it is Hartt's peculiar genius to have found a way to do theology as practical and critical reflection on our cultural practices.

Hartt simply did not seem to fit easily into the boxes used to locate a theologian's work. He clearly was not a protestant liberal, but he did not seem to be a "conservative" either. Some of his work seemed to echo Barth, but his understanding of the importance of philosophy for theology did not seem to square with a Barthian program. Hartt simply went his own way producing an extraordinary theological perspective, but also one that was not fully appreciated because he did not conform to the conventions of the day.

Hartt's work in many ways is more English than American. He was, of course, one of the few American theologians that understood the significance of Austin Farrer's work. But it is also true that Julian was the master of the English essay tradition. His work is not burdened by footnotes because he was never one to think theology consisted in writing about other theologians. He thought that theology was about God and he simply was not going to be distracted by writing about the concept of X in Y. That he wrote so directly, however, meant that many readers found him far too demanding while others simply had no way to understand him.

One of the reasons Julian's work was not widely read was because he was so philosophically sophisticated. Having written his dissertation on Anselm, and in particular Anselm's "proof" for God's existence ("The Ontological Argument for the existence of God: A Historico-Critical Exposition of Some of Its Metaphysical and Epistemological Issues," unpublished Ph.D. dissertation, Yale, 1940), Hartt's work was philosophically informed in a manner that some readers simply could not follow. Julian, moreover, possessed analytical gifts combined with a determined honesty that meant he was never tempted to engage in theology done by slogans. As a result he challenged the simplistic formulas characteristic of theology written for widespread consumption. Given Julian's work on Anselm it is not surprising that he begins *Toward a Theology of Evangelism* with God. He does so because, as he puts it, "the Christian proclamation begins with God, his being and his action. The gospel has something to say about God or it has nothing consequential to say about anything." Hartt, without mentioning Tillich, declares that the "Christian faith does not begin with problems and then look around for their religious solution. To be at all is to be involved with God." Such a claim risked being identified as "Barthian," but Hartt is too much the metaphysician to be so easily labeled. Indeed if any label was to be applied he would have been more justly classified as a Thomist. Of course some of us think that Barth and Aquinas share more in common than is often acknowledged.

Crucial for understanding Hartt is the phrase that follows immediately from his claim that the Christian proclamation begins with God, that is, "his being and his action." Before David Burrell's Wittgensteinian account of Aquinas's understanding of being as action, Hartt had rediscovered that God's being is God's actuality. Only in God are essence and existence one, because only God is able to act without loss. Therefore later in *Toward a Theology of Evangelism* Hartt argues that there is no reason to say that eternity is timeless if you understand that time "is an act, an activity, by which time is constituted and by which it is consummated. Eternity is being which by its own activity sustains all enduring subjects" (105). Of course eternity is, therefore, not a category that precedes our understanding of God, but rather is a predication of God.

Hartt is first and foremost a theologian, but for him theology requires a robust metaphysical imagination. Theology demands the kind of metaphysical work Hartt engages because the subject of theology is God and, accordingly, all existence must be construed under the lordship of God. God is Being, which all people encounter as the absolute limit of the world and themselves, which means that to know anything is to know God. Hartt, therefore, long before Alasdair MacIntyre, refused the epistemological starting point of modern philosophy because he recognized that being precedes knowing. Hartt's theological and philosophical presumptions required him to practice theology on the assumption that no subject is off limits for the theologian. Hartt's metaphysics and his social criticism are but aspects of the same set of theological convictions.

Sounding a theme that has become familiar in theologians such as Nicholas Lash, Rowan Williams, and Denys Turner, Hartt suggests that God is most hidden in his revelation of himself in Jesus. God is no less God for having made himself known, but God's revelation does not mean we, therefore, have a handle on God. Rather, that God refuses to let us go to hell because he loves what he has made means that God is God and we are not. Accordingly, the more we understand of God's creation and redemption the more we understand we have yet to understand the God who would love us.

Hartt develops metaphysical reminders concerning the actuality of being to prepare the way for the story that the church has to tell the nations, that is, that Jesus Christ is the center of the Christian faith. Hartt's account of Jesus, however, is informed by his metaphysics. Jesus is what Jesus does. He is the supreme witness to the kingdom of God through which God's faithfulness is enacted so that we may know that God's desire is to have us for himself. Hartt, therefore, does not extensively use the language of "incarnation." Jesus is, of course, the incarnate Word, the Son of God, but Hartt is careful not to let the language of incarnation make secondary Jesus' enactment of the kingdom in his miracles, teaching, crucifixion, and resurrection. Jesus, for Hartt, is at once the one who proclaims the kingdom and the one who is the kingdom. Accordingly, Jesus is not a set of ideas but the concrete actuality of the kingdom. That actuality means that a community of the reconciled must exist or otherwise salvation is ephemeral. But "resurrection is the creation of salvation, the final historical sign that the new community is now in our midst and that Jesus Christ is the Lord of this Life. This same Jesus Christ is thus shown forth as the Lord of history" (35).

I have tried to make candid what I take to be Hartt's strategy in the first part of *Toward a Theology of Evangelism*, but I confess I am not sure I understand why Hartt develops an account of the human situation before he deals with the Spirit and the church. Hartt is clearly intent to avoid the liberal protestant mistake of making theology primarily an account of the human condition. He well knows that such a strategy cannot avoid Feuerbach. Yet Hartt quite rightly thinks that theology has a stake in what he will call in *The Christian Critique of American Culture* the ontological essentials of the human condition—death, love, creativity, anxiety, guilt. Civilization is the name for the particular forms of life shaped by these invariables. So Hartt's anthropology involves his theological engagement with cultural formations.

Hartt may well have thought it important, therefore, to develop his understanding of the human situation prior to developing his account of the Spirit and the church because it provided him with the opportunity to stress the centrality of history for the display of the actuality of our lives. "History is what man has done to himself," which is but a way to say that we are subject to sin. I confess I do worry a bit that Hartt seems to think he can give an account of sin prior to salvation, but his understanding of sin as the "indictment against existence as history" is surely an appropriate way to highlight our prideful attempt to deny the contingency of our created status.

His analysis of the human situation is a prelude to his account of the actuality of redemption by the foundation of an actual community through the Spirit. The name of that community is "church." The church's task is not to witness to herself, but to the Kingdom established by the Son of God. Through her witness to the Kingdom the church at once stands in and against the world. God's salvation, the Kingdom of God, is a revolution creating for us an otherwise unavailable way to live in the world. Accordingly, the revolution that is the Kingdom is more profound than any revolutions the world can offer because the church challenges all social structures built and justified on the presumption that they represent eternity.

The church, like all things human, is not immune from the pride that besets all worldly institutions. But the church, nonetheless, is the arena of sanctification as a communal process that will also include the lives of individuals. Hartt observes: "the church is not to be thought of, therefore, as the place where people are miraculously shorn of their sins. It is the place where, by the miracle of Christ's love, people learn to take deepening responsibility for other sinners." I shall leave it to others to judge if Hartt's understanding of sanctification is or is not compatible with Wesley's account of perfection.

I have tried to outline what I take to be the main structure of the theology Hartt develops to provide an account of evangelism. Some may wonder, however, what or why his understanding of theology is necessary for the evangelical task of the church. Hartt's answer is quite straightforward. His theological work helps us understand that the church is evangelical by her very existence. The church's task is to proclaim that the Kingdom of

God is present in Jesus, the Son of God. So the evangelical task is not something "else" the church may do. It is what the church is and does.

Hartt, therefore, critiques those who have confused the gospel with cultural idealities. Remember Hartt is writing in the early years of the cold war. The church will rightly have cultural effects, but it is a deep mistake to confuse the gospel with a defense of American democracy against Communism. Indeed it is a deep mistake to confuse the church with America.

"A certificate for meritorious service on behalf of civilization is not to be mistaken for the church's charter." You cannot say it more clearly than Hartt said it in 1955. Evangelism, therefore, is not a strategy for drawing more people into the churches. Rather evangelism is the proclamation of the message: "This is the acceptable year of the Lord; repent, for the Kingdom of God is at hand!" This proclamation is not something the church does over and above other things she is called to do, but this is the central work of the church, which means that the church is part of the proclamation to the world. Hartt's theological account of evangelism, moreover, provides him with the resources to develop a biting critique of "evangelistic tactics." The church has been given a holy task—to proclaim the Kingdom of perfect love—but the church has betrayed that task by cheerfully adopting the devices and gimmicks that are the tricks of the huckster and the salesman. Accordingly, "what the church has to 'sell' must be something that can be put in a cheerful and attractive package. The church's product must be obviously usable to the point of indispensability and far beyond. The minister also must show that he is a good manager, a real executive." In short, in 1955 Hartt had diagnosed how evangelism had been confused with the attempt to maintain the status of the church by making the church the chaplain of the established order. His analysis and critique of evangelistic methods is as relevant to our current situation as it was to the world Hartt saw so clearly was beginning.

Evangelism is the church's ongoing task to distinguish between worldly time and the time of the Kingdom. She does that by exhibiting the significance of the nearness of the Kingdom for how our lives are structured by work, play, and love. Christians believe that God has given us all the time we need to be in love. To love is to be freed from our illusions made possible by the actuality of the Kingdom that is now. The church's witness to the Kingdom is called worship for it is through worship we catch a vision of a peace that the world neither knows nor can take away. So runs the argument Hartt develops in *Toward a Theology of Evangelism*. Some may think, however, that the account I have given sounds more like Hauerwas than Hartt. But it really is Hartt and if the position I have outlined sounds like Hauerwas it is only a testimony to how much I learned from Hartt. I took his systematic theology course the first year I entered seminary. I cannot pretend I understood everything that was going on in the course, but I am sure I learned some of the basic theological moves that have from the beginning informed the way I have tried to do theology.

I am equally sure, moreover, that I decided to be an "ethicist" because of what I learned from Hartt's course. For I was convinced by Hartt that the truthfulness of theological discourse was to be tested by its power to construe the world. Accordingly, I was determined to show that to make a strong distinction between theory and practice is a mistake. So I became an "ethicist" in order to practice theology in a manner I had learned from Julian Hartt. I should like to think, moreover, that Julian might recognize some of what he taught me in the way I have worked.

At the very least I hope this "Introduction" may help some discover that Hartt's work remains as powerful for the challenges facing the church today as it was when it was written. Indeed my hope is that we may now be in a position to appreciate and appropriate Hartt's work in a more fruitful way than when his books were first published. Hartt was a creative theological voice because he desired to be faithful to the gospel. As a result he did not have the influence he deserved. Of course because he was faithful to the gospel he was not concerned that his work lacked influence. But hopefully we may now be in a position to read *Toward a Theology of Evangelism* and recognize the power of Hartt's work for the challenges before us.

—Stanley Hauerwas, 2006
Duke University

CONTENTS

I. A Charge to Keep 9

II. God, the Almighty Father 13

III. Our Lord, Jesus Christ 26

IV. The Human Situation 42

V. The Holy Spirit and the Church 60

VI. The World and the Kingdom 67

VII. World Revolution and
Individual Transformation 76

VIII. Evangelical Zeal and Cultural Pride 88

IX. The Race with Time 98

X. The Living Word in Our Midst 113

Index 121

I

A Charge to Keep

> "*Go therefore and make disciples of all nations.*" —Matt. 28:19

From the beginning the Christian community has felt an irresistible compulsion to publish its message to all mankind, under the conviction that this message is the word of life for all men. The people of this community are profoundly convinced that this message was not of the church's own devising: the church was created by the living Word uttered through it. Created so, the Christian community has a divine commission to be only and purely the humble servant of the Word, declaring unto the ends of the earth and until the end of time the good news concerning the kingdom of God.

Wherever the church is authentically Christian the conviction yet lives that its sole reason for existence is to preach the gospel of the kingdom in Christ. The commission is there held to be still in force, the commission to "evangelize the world." But great are the difficulties in holding this conviction purely and firmly, and the difficulties multiply daily. Each day sees the task grown more complex, and the dangers grow with the complexities. Our world seems more deeply and systematically immunized against the gospel than ever before. And yet in this world the church is frequently hailed as a great, indeed perhaps the greatest, defender of Western democratic civilization. The church preaches God as the Father and Redeemer of all men and of the whole man. And yet even in the church obedience to this God is effectively represented as a fractional and marginal claim, if it is accepted as a serious claim at all. The church is chartered and commissioned to perform a holy task—the proclamation of the Kingdom of perfect love and perfect freedom. And yet this same church is fiercely competitive for its share of loyalty, and to assure the same it cheerfully adopts promotional devices, gimmicks and angles which in our day are the hallmarks of the huckster, the pusher, the super-salesman.

Dismayed by the depth and profusion of problems in our civilization and affronted by shabby evangelisms within the church, many good Christian people are wondering whether the evangelical commission of the church has not been outgrown or outworn. Does it not sometimes appear to us that the solemn charge laid upon the original Christian community has been finally discharged—has not the entire world now heard about the kingdom of Christ? Does it not also seem to us that to carry out the charge leads naturally and inevitably to ecclesiastical imperialism and thence to all of the vices and iniquities of intolerance, totalitarianism, and rampant bigotry? History is rich with evidence to support affirmative answers to the latter question, as our own complacency and fear may well produce a "yes" to the former.

But the decision is not so simple. We honor Christ as Lord. How then shall we reject his commandment, his charge? How shall we take thought to reduce that charge to inanity and triviality? These dire things we can try to do only so far as first we are minded to write our own gospel and to create a Christ after the desires of our own hearts. We must interpret the gospel, to be sure, and we profess that Christ is in our hearts; but the gospel itself is given to us, not by the past, but by the living Lord who reigns in our hearts. And out of the gospel so given, the obligation to evangelize the world arises to claim our acceptance and our obedience. To this obligation every Christian believer, and every fellowship of believers, brings his own patterns of compulsions and aspirations. These compulsions and aspirations bring us—drive us, rather—to Christ; but they do not of themselves determine what or whom we encounter in him. And there is the redeeming possibility that in his service something more than our fears and our hopes will be communicated to others.

As Christians we cannot let go of the evangelical commission. As people of this time we cannot hope to face and to fulfill its demands unless we grasp anew that actuality upon which our Christian existence is established and which constitutes the inner life of the church. That actuality is everlasting. It is revealed in history, but it is not confined in the past and its power and its glory do not depend upon the reconstruction of the past through memory and creative imagination. That actuality has elicited historical record—scripture; but without the ongoing life in the church the scriptural record would take final and undisturbing place in the library of the world's classics. There is much in the church's life, as there is much in our civilization, which would be gratified were scripture so entombed. God wills otherwise. That to which scripture witnesses is a present and wholly concrete actuality, present and concrete in the past, present and concrete now. Therefore, our task is not to conjure this actuality out of the past but to apprehend its presently real and everlasting character and its real demands upon us. In so conceiving the matter we act conformably to the mind of the New Testament, since in the New Testament little attention is directed simply to the remembrance of things past, and, so far as attention is directed to this, it is for the sake of a deeper apprehension of present actuality, and for a steadier expectation of a future unutterably rich with divine fulfillments. May it be so with us.

TOWARD A THEOLOGY OF EVANGELISM

We would face up to the demands of the evangelical commission. Therefore, ministering to our time, we must reflect in all seriousness upon the fundamentals of Christian existence. And this reflection must occur in the working and praying church. We cannot strip away our love and our anxiety for that fellowship in order to meditate coolly and abstractly about the meaning of life in general. It is in the church that we know about God who is the Father of our Lord Jesus Christ, and it is here that we are encouraged and enabled to accept certain imperatives and to grasp certain possibilities as desirable above all others. The obligations so accepted and the possibilities so envisaged and aspired after may turn out to be significant points of productive contact with people outside the church altogether, but we know they are also the signs of certainty for the believer himself. To be bound by such duties and to be enraptured by such possibilities are fruits of the Holy Spirit.

What follows is something by way of reflection upon fundamentals of Christian existence, reflection inspired by the desire to grasp the meaning of the church's commission. The discerning reader will see quickly enough that this is not a systematic theology. It is biblical theology only in the rarefied sense that it may suggest an effort to apprehend and to interpret the actualities to which scripture bears witness. But it is not theology at all if that term suggests an announcement or a declaration of conclusive results and findings. We seek a country and we march in the light of truth which we love and have not in us as our own; for we are not our own but his who bears this witness to himself: "I am the Truth."

II

God, the Almighty Father

THE MOST FAMILIAR CREED OF THE CHURCH BEGINS: "I BElieve in God the Father Almighty, Maker of heaven and earth." It is entirely appropriate that the creed should begin at this point, for this is indeed the first proposition of Christian belief and the theological foundation of Christian experience.

The Christian proclamation begins with God, his being and his action. The gospel has something to say about God or it has nothing consequential to say about anything. It does have something to say about man, too; but in the gospel man is what he is because God is God. There we learn that man is not first aware of his own situation and then anxious or curious to discover whether anything exists to cure it. In the Christian faith man does not begin with problems and then look around for their religious solution. To be at all is to be involved with God. Who or what is this God? The Christian faith declares that God is the "Almighty Father who liveth unto himself." God has being beyond the world, not as an ideal or as a possibility, but as one who actually and fully is. The phrase "God the Father" rightly arouses images of a profoundly solicitous Deity, but it is certainly not intended to suggest that God is a domesticated subject or servant of the world and man. Rather, God is "only Sovereign, the King of kings and Lord of lords, who alone has immortality and dwells in unapproachable light, whom no man has ever seen or can see" (I Tim. 6:15-16).

What dealings do we creatures of the dust have with so great a God? We cannot fail to encounter him, and deal with him we must. All men encounter him first as the awful negation of all finitude. God is the formidable unbroken silence enshrouding the noises of ephemeral creatures. In such knowledge there is no salvation and no hint or promise of salvation, except perhaps from any illusion that we are more than creature. But how different this universal knowledge of God from what passed under that name in ages less profoundly troubled than ours! That knowledge of God common to all people was then what one could reasonably surmise of Deity from the evidences of the intelligent and presumptively benign ordering of nature and of human affairs. What a change of heart and mind separates the men of this generation from that comfortable illusion! Know ye not in your hearts that God alone is God? Aye, we know, and knowing, we tremble, for we have had a dark encounter with God. We have discovered again the fear of the Lord; and now we know that the fear of the Lord is part of our very nature, as it is the beginning of wisdom. The world is ultimately mysterious, not piquantly, but formidably mysterious. It is a place of glad surprise; it is also a place of shattering terror; and in both it is God's world.

While many people wonder today why these fundamental realities of the human condition under God were so recently concealed and distorted in their understanding, there are others for whom the rose-colored mists of religious sentimentality and of sentimental religion have not been entirely burned away even yet. Wisps and tatters of these comforting fogs float gently through the church and have some continuing success in swathing and muffling the worship and witness of the church. But the mists are being

GOD, THE ALMIGHTY FATHER

burned away. The actualities are catching up with us. Cultural cateclysms shatter our peace, blow upon blow, shock upon shock. An abyss opens at our feet. Heaven is no longer a dreamy and restful blue—it is brassy and hard and ominous. The terror that stalks the world at noonday has also found its way into our street, and we can neither escape it nor master it.

Who then speaks most powerfully to and for the men of this generation? Those poets, artists, and philosophers who preach despair and sing of bleak encounter with silence and futility and nonbeing. And what shall we pious ones say about their utterance? We must say that it speaks of God, and that the God to whom they bear witness is not such a one as we would love to create in our own image! We would not dream or dare to dream of capturing and domesticating that God by some shrewd act of self-abasement and calculated humility.

The God whom it is wisdom to fear has powerful and courageous witnesses outside the church. To encounter this God and to be engaged with him is a deadly serious matter. And from this mortal engagement comes a fierce contempt for the genteel and conventional demigods of our day—those companionable household deities of a people withdrawn as far as humanly possible from the raw frontiers of existence. These demigods are ubiquitous. In richly carpeted and decorous funeral parlors they whisper soothingly. They flit and flicker in our minds when disaster overtakes us, and they seduce us with comfortable and ingratiating sentiments. When we despair, they whisper that every cloud has a silver lining. When we would sit in sackcloth and cover our heads with ashes for our sins, they gently reprove us for thinking more poorly of ourselves than we ought to think. These demigods of the mist have been our companions and our masters; and in their service we have hoped to find peace of mind. But when the chips are down, half-gods evaporate. And the chips are down. If we people of the church are only vaguely aware that this is so, it is perhaps because the demigods still confuse and bedazzle us. In this respect the "heathen" in our midst may be more mature religiously than we are. When this is so, evangelism has its problems—among the targets of the program must be the truly inspired atheists who know that half-gods do not exist!

God is Being which all men encounter as the absolute limitation of the world and themselves. To know that this God is, makes no demands upon faith, so far, and requires no churchly sanction. God as this Being we may identify as pure transcendence.[1] But God as pure transcendence is more than boundary and negation of creaturely existence. God is the ultimate basis of every creaturely existence. He is the positive foundation for all that we do and for all that we know. If, then, we grasp anything as true, whether it is trivial or sublime, it is God's doing. Therefore, to know anything at all is to know God. What I know of self, of other-self, of nature, I know in and through God's being. God is that light through which all things are beheld, so far as our minds are capable of grasping them.[2]

---

[1] This does not mean that God is "far-off" or "somewhere above the world." Transcendence as a theological concept has to do with perfection of being and power apart from anything other than God. "Immanence," on the other hand, has to do with immediate efficacy of operation, as the soul, for example, can be said to be immanent in the body; so far as the mind enjoys an immediate efficacy of operation in relation to the brain, it does not achieve its effects through the co-operation of some mediating agency. Hence, for God to be immanent in the world in no sense implies a loss of the divine perfection of being.

[2] Supernatural ingenuity of intellect is not really required to extract from this fundamental intuition of divine being a proof for God's existence. No great harm is visited upon either piety or philosophical dignity by such an exercise, unless its intention is grossly misunderstood. People do say sometimes that the pious are beyond any need for such exercise and that the philosophers are beyond any help from it. It is possible that these people

GOD, THE ALMIGHTY FATHER

God is Being in whom alone truth is possible and actual. Here we are learning, all of us, a hard and bitter lesson: the truth is not necessarily lovable. Indeed, the more profoundly disillusioned among us feel, and powerfully proclaim, that the truth, the whole truth and the truth about the whole, is more nearly hateful and horrid than lovable. We do not all see it this way, but we cannot fail to see that God the Transcendent, in whom all creatures live and move and have their being, is utterly beyond our normal notions of good and evil. That is why we tremble before him. He who sets boundaries to every creature and who overcomes the world, is not *nothing*, is not a limitless void. We do not die away before a mere cipher. As the poet says, "All things die and pass away," but they are crowded and shouldered out of the way by something more powerful. As for ourselves, also, we do not lose to death; we lose everywhere and always to life. Our life-and-death struggle is with Being inexhaustively fecund: and its boundless creativity mocks our public and our private schemes of good and evil. And so we tremble before God the Transcendent, all-terrible in his creativity. He shows no regard for the moral schemes of his creatures. He shows no solicitude for the moral schemes of civilizations and nations, rich and poor, great and small. Every creature and every creaturely achievement is born under sentence; and there is no commutation, no time off for good behavior, and no pardon.

Slowly but surely we are coming around to see the actualities of our situation as human and creaturely. Reluctantly we are beginning to see the actualities of our situation as members of Western civilization and as Ameri-

---

overlook the copresence of piety and philosophy here and there; or, if they see this, they may say it is impossible; and here, as elsewhere, the sturdy insistence that fact is impossible is rich with comic possibilities.

can. Our social order, our way of life, even though we say they are the darling of God's eye, will yield to some other order; and no man knows the hour thereof. There is left to us not even the harsh comfort of supposing that the aftermath of the atomic war will be a world denuded of all significant human life. Human life will go on trying to come to terms with an outraged nature and with the radically altered possibilities of humanity. Our civilization may go up in flames and never rise again from the ashes. But something will come on after us. Whether it will be nobler than what we have created, or otherwise, who shall say, or in saying reveal anything but pride and horror?

It is with real seriousness, therefore, that we have learned again to say that God's ways are not our ways. God the Transcendent does not think as we think. He brings forth a multitude of things that irritate and imperil mankind; and he has thrown all of them and all of us and other progeny too numerous and perchance too hideous to mention into the same world; and he marks none as his favorite. God sends his rains upon the just and the unjust alike. He gives men and streptococci alike a full lease on life; and he does not tip the scale arbitrarily in favor of one or against the other. We are free to attack and destroy as many streptococci as we will; and they are free to resist us and to destroy as many of us as they can; and neither is given a clear edge, a metaphysical fast start, over the other.

So absolute a lack of discrimination in God oppresses us sometimes to the vestibule of madness. We fight back against this madness of despair by saying our prayers with renewed fervor, but this fervor cannot silence the question whether God the Transcendent would heed our prayers. Or perhaps we write theologies, hoping thus to dull someone's pain at any rate, but we secretly fear that God himself has already refuted all our theological answers. Or we may try to build a barrier against this madness by engaging in

GOD, THE ALMIGHTY FATHER

febrile social activity, as in church life, P.T.A., and Odd Fellows.

This picture is of course partial and one-sided. It leaves out our Christian belief that in his own way God does discriminate: he is forever on the side of justice and forever opposed to injustice. Alas, this does little to balance the picture or to sweeten the potion, for what are justice and injustice in God's sight? What does God do to establish the just and to unseat the unjust? In this acutely critical hour for our common life and for our private sanity and peace, we find ourselves yearning for a dramatic and overpowering disclosing of God's righteousness. Oh, how we search the heavens and the horizons for the manifest power and glory of the Kingdom! Come quickly, Lord! But the Lord tarries in heaven. Disconsolate, we pick up cold stones for bread —we say to one another that the wicked, the monstrous evil ones, can win only in the short run.

> "Brief and violent is their day:
> Then they wither and pass away."

Hitler screeched the obscene glory of his thousand-year empire, but within five years he was dead, a rat in his own trap, while overhead his empire went up in flame. But what of Jesus, who came doing good and preaching the holy glory of the eternal Kingdom of divine love? Within three years he was dead, hung on a cross by a venal Roman administrator. And the empire so poorly represented by Pontius Pilate *did* endure, all told, for a thousand years. Thus the truth is pressed into our vitals: the inclusive scheme of things, the moral order of the universe, is clearly not like a decently maintained neighborhood. God is not like the friendly cop on the corner of that neighborhood, one

TOWARD A THEOLOGY OF EVANGELISM

pocket filled with goodies for the kids and the other with bullets for the mad dogs, human and otherwise, that might frighten or endanger the neighborhood. The inclusive scheme of things is God's, and it is no neighborhood. The divine scheme has little to do with all our mortal schemes of good and evil, except, upon unpredictable occasion, to crush them as a ten-ton truck crushes a child's pretty tinkling bauble that rolls under its wheels.

People beyond the church know these things about God the Transcendent. These people may not express themselves in the words we have been using, but they have confronted the actualities signified. Surely the church is not commissioned to tell these people what they already know, and just as surely the church has no business trying to persuade them that the truth they grasp isn't so. Furthermore, the evangelical task is not to sell them church language with which to express the actualities of the common human situation under God. What then? The church bears witness to God's revelation. It preaches God the Revealer. And it preaches that God the Revealer and God the Transcendent are one God. Who will say that the evangelical commission is an easy yoke? But only so far as the church knows God as Revealer can it rightly claim to be ordained and commissioned for specific tasks. For to be ordained means to be designated by God for a specific mission dear to God's heart. If God makes specific designations and thereby evinces a regard for his creatures, he reveals activities and interests in himself not at all discoverable in purely transcendent being. That is why we must say that if the church is truly called, it is because and only because God truly reveals himself.

When the Christian says that God is Revealer, he certainly has in mind some of the day-to-day meaning of the word "revelation." To "reveal" is to make an intimate

GOD, THE ALMIGHTY FATHER

disclosure of oneself to another person—in human relationships revelation is always a person-to-person transaction. So understood, revelation is not merely another item of knowledge to be added into a composite body of other items of knowledge. A revelation is an authoritative and decisive disclosure-and-comprehension of a whole pattern, a whole life. When I say that what John X said or did yesterday was a revelation to me, I mean to say that a whole pattern came to unity and light in a decisive and compelling way. We say, therefore, that what is *revealed* stands in the mind and heart of the recipient in a relationship of peculiar immediacy and power. If we say, then, that God reveals himself, we mean that at such and such a point or in such and such a way he stands in the minds and hearts of some persons in a relationship of peculiar immediacy and power. Accordingly, what is so apprehended of God is not another item of knowledge to be added into a composite body of other items of knowledge concerning God. The other items of knowledge are not cancelled, for that matter, by God's revelation; they are taken up into a new unity and a new life. God the Revealer does not supercede God the Transcendent: we do well to fear the Lord, but we do better to adore him; for God reveals himself as the Father Almighty.

Revelation does not make all things of God known. We cannot "read him like an open book." He makes himself known, but for all of that, and in all of that, he is yet unknown. This theme has had many formulations in Christian history. Perhaps the most vivid of these is that God reveals himself as the "hidden God"—God revealed is God concealed. Now when paradox leaps out at us so fiercely, we quite understandably rebuke it or scuttle for safety. Yet the paradox reveals—and conceals—a truth we should not try to escape: God is no less God for his having made himself known, for no action of God can conceivably involve a diminution or depreciation of his own being. To enter into immediate and intimate dealings with his creatures entails no abdication of his power and right.[3]

God reveals himself as the absolute and free bestower of being. All things show forth his handiwork: whatever is, owes its whole being to God. God freely bestows being. He is the giver of life. Wherefore, there is a unique relation of everything and all things to God: all depend absolutely upon him. And this holds as fully for us human creatures as it does for any other creature. We may be created in God's image; but we are creatures, and not God. Whatever we are and have is a gift; and since God is wholly free in giving, we can hardly say of anything we have or aspire after, that God *ought* to respect or provide it. God goes abroad with life and light, but not because of some compulsion or constraint.

God reveals himself as the light of our minds. God is "light unapproachable," but he is also the "true light that enlightens every man coming into the world." God the Revealer is the light of the mind and the light of the world. As it was put before, anything we know, we know through the intimate operation in our minds of truth beyond our minds. Now let us put it this way: this truth is not an impersonal operation any more than it is a lifeless realm of being; it is the action of God the Revealer. In this we are saying that God's actions, indeed, his very being, are intimately and immediately involved with our actions and our being. Without him we can do nothing; without him we are nothing. But we must also say that what we are and do

[3] As "revelation" is interpreted above, the hiddenness of God is, precisely, not revealed but is an immediate datum: the hiddenness of God is grasped essentially by all men; and, in our time, it is better remembered outside the church—the community of revelation—than within it.

concerns God, because God is the Revealer. He is not a detached and remote observer of the world. He is essentially involved with the world. God is bound to his creation and to his creatures by the strongest of all ties: God *loves* the world.

So we are brought to the affirmation: God the Father Almighty reveals himself as the Redeemer. Sometimes the church preaches redemption as if it were a divine repair and patch-up job, followed by an everlasting convalescence. In the New Testament and in productive Christian experience always, the actualities are very differently comprehended. There God the Redeemer is encountered as the One who promises "a new heaven and a new earth," and as the One in whom "all things have become new." God the Redeemer bestows new being upon us creatures—this is the whole work of redemption.

The future can be faced with hope and earnest expectation only because God the Transcendent is also God self-revealed as Redeemer. Had we to reckon only with God as the negation of all finitude, we were without hope and great expectations. In their place we could perhaps await a mood and a poetic fancy with which to pay compliments to the sheer ongoingness of things in general—we like sometimes to think it rather magnificent that the world refuses to lie down and die when we lie down and die. But these moods flicker off and on, and the poetic fancies are fickle; and altogether there is little of the substance of actuality in them, as our own time and spirit testify. Nature alone can only cheat expectations she has not herself elicited. The hunger for the higher righteousness, the earnest expectations of the creatures, the groanings and travailings of creation— these lead straight and full beyond nature and beyond ourselves to God the Father Almighty. He who is the absolute limitation of all creatures is also the absolute affirmation of all. It is true: death is ordained for all things. But God, not death, is Lord; and death he will finally destroy. It is little to be wondered at therefore that a poet says:

> In my nostrils there is the odor
> Of Death and Dissolution;
> But there is also the fragrance
> Of an eternal Spring.

Through the Revealer we know that "we live and move and have our being" in God (Acts 17:28). God the Almighty Father is closer to us than breathing, nearer than hands and feet—"he is the light of my life, my shield, and my salvation." In these ways and in countless others, the actualities of God's full relations with us have been portrayed.

Faith in God the Father Almighty is the foundation of Christian life and thought, and it is therefore the first principle of the church's evangelical mission. It is the foundation, but it is not the whole faith; and by itself it could not account for the evangelical mission. These foundational convictions are indispensable to the essential life and work of the church, and without them the church cuts and trims its message to conform to the "philosophy and empty deceit" of the world (Col. 2:8). Nevertheless, these primary convictions are too general and too sketchy to hold the whole story and to disclose the really binding part of the story. Indeed, the gospel as story does not appear at all in them. What so far appears is a kind of metaphysical background of the story and for the story. The background must be there. But if the church had only the metaphysical background, it would have no truly divine mission in and for the world. It would have a metaphysics to promulgate, but there is no salvation in metaphysics. To be sure, a social philosophy and a manifesto for social action may be extracted from the metaphysics, and somehow viewed

GOD, THE ALMIGHTY FATHER

as its vindication. This has been done often enough. When the church does it, the church falls into one or the other of twin monumental errors: the substitution of a plausible world view for revelation; or authoritarianism. An authoritarian church is a church in self-contradiction. As for the other error, the world-viewing mentality is more concerned by far with a theory about history than it is with concrete history as the realm of revelation. If the church has but a theory about history as a prime concern, it has no divine mission. The church's mission in and for the world roots in a concrete history. In this concrete history God shows himself forth as acting; and he acts therein in such a way that it becomes absolutely desirable and absolutely imperative that what he has done should be made known to the whole world. God acts: and whoever knows that he is grasped by this action becomes overpoweringly aware of the command, "Go and tell!" This is the fate of the church; it can be resisted, but it cannot be eluded.

The mission of the church demands sacrifice in the highest degree. Such sacrifice ought not be made in the interest of a world view or a metaphysics, whatever it entails, any more than such sacrifice ought to be made in the interests of the temporal power and grandeur of the church. Such sacrifice should be made only for creating and enhancing a concrete situation involving persons, a situation which God consecrates and which therefore promises the fullest and widest fulfillment of human possibilities. The sacrifice of self for the spreading of the gospel is aimed at that concrete situation which is the kingdom of God. God acts to reveal that Kingdom to us and to bring it into our midst.

III

Our Lord, Jesus Christ

THE CHURCH HAS A "STORY TO TELL TO THE NATIONS." THE story tells that God the Father Almighty has acted in history for all mankind. What is it he has done? God has established a community, a "kingdom," and he calls all men freely to participate in the life of this community for the fulfillment of his promises and of man's great expectations. These things God has done through Jesus Christ, his only begotten Son, our Lord.

In the New Testament this concrete historical actuality, Jesus Christ, is interpreted in three ways of primary importance for our reflection: Jesus Christ is the supreme witness to the kingdom of God; Jesus Christ is the incarnate Lord, the crown prince and heir of the Kingdom; Jesus Christ is the Kingdom.

The second and third of these interpretations are natural and inevitable expansions of the first, given the apprehended realities of Christian experience. They grow out of and beyond the first, not by a process of logical derivation but by further experiences with and further reflection upon the concrete actualities themselves, which are continuously and dynamically revealed to faith. Because the first of these enjoys a real primacy in the church's history, we shall devote considerably more time to it in this discussion.

1. The first line of testimony concerning Jesus Christ is that he is the supreme witness to the kingdom of God.

OUR LORD, JESUS CHRIST

This is set forth in the following ways: Jesus Christ is the assurance of God's faithfulness; Jesus Christ himself takes the proclamation of the kingdom of God to be his divinely sanctioned mission, in respect to its righteousness, its immanence, and the urgency of its demands; Jesus Christ the Witness has in himself the power of God the Father Almighty. Jesus Christ is the full assurance of God's faithfulness in covenant and promise. This assurance he brings to the people whose entire historical existence was determined by covenant and promise. The people of the New Testament community testify that Jesus Christ has done certain things before their very eyes in which the fulfillment of the divine promise is made perfectly clear. What has been promised is the kingdom of God, that divine-human community in which suffering and death are overcome in absolute finality, and the peace of God crowns the powers of spirit and of nature. In the Old Testament peace, power, and prosperity are quite characteristically dramatized as salient features of this community. Even in the highly idealized messianic poems of Isaiah the prosperity and productivity of the Kingdom are vividly portrayed.[1] These aspects of life in the Kingdom are not ignored in the New Testament; there too it is understood that power and glory pertain to the Kingdom, though not as the world reckons

---

[1] "The wilderness and the dry land shall be glad,
    the desert shall rejoice and blossom;
like the crocus it shall blossom abundantly,
    and rejoice with joy and singing.
. . . .
The abundance of the sea shall be turned to you,
    the wealth of the nations shall come to you.
. . . .
They shall bring gold and frankincense,
    and shall proclaim the praise of the Lord.
All the flocks of Kedar shall be gathered to you. . . ."
                                    Isa. 35:1-2; 60:5, 6, 7

them and not as Israel had conceived them. And in the New Testament it is also understood that the peace of the Kingdom impinges upon men first of all as the demand for repentance and then as the quite incredible promise of redemption from obedience to demonic powers. Israel expects the Kingdom to come; but the Kingdom that comes no one expects; and when it comes, it overcomes our alienation from God and our alienation from one another.

In the Synoptic Gospels, Jesus Christ asserts as his divine mission the proclamation of this kingdom of God (cf. Luke 4:16-21). As he reveals the Kingdom, we are compelled to see that its righteousness is beyond all conventional morality, whether the most scrupulously conscientious morality of piety or a more worldly morality. The righteousness that issues from pious scrupulosity may be worlds away from the purity and single-minded obedience which the living God demands.[2] But the love demanded by the Kingdom, and which is possible only in the Kingdom, is utterly beyond all worldly and egoistic tactics and strategies whereby we hope to wrest advantage for self from all others and achieve, if possible, positive possession of them and mastery over their destinies. Hence, we cannot be mistaken: the righteousness of exploitive morality is also infinitely remote from the righteousness of the Kingdom of absolute love. The same is true of every attempted synthesis of the moralities of scrupulous piety and worldly exploitation: we may mask our self-aggrandizing moves with pious gestures, but God is not taken in. Our chagrin matches that of the sons of Zebedee when we too at last discover that in the Kingdom there is no place for any of our clever and deadly jockeying for power and prestige! Love without the impetus to overpower, to

---

[2] "For I tell you, unless your righteousness exceeds that of the scribes and Pharisees, you will never enter the kingdom of heaven." (Matt. 5:20.) Clearly, "exceeds" doesn't mean a more intense form of the same morality—it means a different kind of morality altogether.

master, and to play the lord to subjects suppliant for our favors? Is this not a denial of our competitive natures? Is there not some effective way of bringing injunction against such subversion?

Jesus Christ reveals that the peace, power, and beauty of the kingdom of God are unlike anything that any worldly kingdom can seriously promise. In his revealing we see that his Kingdom cannot be taken by storm. It cannot be seized; we can only pray, with an importunity directly related to our apprehension of its blessed actuality, that it should come on earth. And here Jesus Christ reveals something further of the Kingdom: it does come, it is exerting imperious pressure upon the world. It is bearing downwards and inwards upon us. This pressure and weight of the Kingdom are very different from the attraction of a noble possibility —the Kingdom is a mighty power, invincible in its perfect actuality. It comes in "majestic instancy"; it tarries not; and there is no time to lose and no place to hide. The kingdom of God is at hand: therefore, repent!

In this demand for immediate and full repentance all that Jesus declared concerning the Kingdom is represented, for only through repentance can one hope to enter the Kingdom. The boon of the Kingdom: forgiveness of sins. The time of the Kingdom: now. The categorical imperative: decide!

This imperative sense of urgency was communicated to the disciples and to the early church. Where the church is faithful yet to its Lord and to its charter, a profound and unshakable sense of urgency in the proclamation of the Kingdom remains. To be sure, this urgency has been misunderstood and misappropriated many times. In our time we confuse it with all kinds of worldly anxieties, just as we are prone to confuse the glory of the Kingdom with the prestige of the church. We are also tempted to explain away the instancy of the Kingdom as a natural mistake of minds saturated with apocalypticism. But to drain off or to neutralize the instancy and urgency of the Kingdom is to lose touch with the concrete actualities in which Christian faith is grounded and to which the church must look if it is to have a legitimate confidence in truth and power—the truth and power of the gospel.

New Testament Christianity also affirms that Jesus Christ the Witness has in himself the power of God the Father Almighty. There are four ways in which this power of God is revealed in Jesus Christ: the miracles, the teaching, the forgiving of sins, the Resurrection. Let us briefly consider each of these.

In the New Testament the miracles, and notably the miracles of healing and exorcism, are regarded as direct demonstrations of the power of God working, and in some sense resident, in Jesus Christ (cf. Luke 11:20). In the Synoptics, Jesus is shown launching a full-scale attack upon the demonic powers which afflict and harass mankind. According to Acts, this power was bestowed upon the apostolic community. The New Testament evinces little curiosity in the question how the demons were cast out. The great thing is that they were expelled and that this was done by "the finger of God," as the demons themselves confess. To deliver human life from their foul servitude is a work of the Kingdom; and the chief executor of that work is the Messiah himself.

The revelation of Christ's power over demons oppresses the children of modernity nearly as much as it afflicted the demons. This mental discomfort occasioned by his mastery over the nether and upper powers of evil is partly justified—we ought to resist stoutly any compulsion to recover the cosmological appetites and anxieties of the New Testament age. This compulsion is presented with unslaked zeal by biblical literalists of many stripes and hues. But the will in us to resist idealists and sentimentalists has been somewhat less sturdy and somewhat less effective. Consequently, we have given careful consideration to the possibility that the demonic is an illusion—all that really is, is good, so runs our modern doctrine. We have also nodded sage approval when it was proposed that "the demonic" is a name for brutish impulses crawling about in the slime of the racial unconscious, and yielding slowly to the persuasions of civilization. But when we hear that "demon possession" is but a New Testament name for what we more properly and soberly identify as severe neurotic symptoms or even galloping psychosis, our cup runneth over; and we leap gladly to appropriate the image of Jesus Christ the Superpsychiatrist. What a heaven-sent key to the mind of the times! [3]

The idealisms and the sentimentalisms which latterly ruled the life of the church have had a rough ride in the contemporary world. In our present situation we are far readier than we were but a short while ago to see that the New Testament apprehension of the demonic is an apprehension of something so fearfully actual and potent that God himself enters the lists against it. The little threadbare illusions of living in a nice-neighborhood-world in which the gravest problems yield to sweet solution in the next chapter of our favorite suds saga, are strictly soiled merchandise. Will the church peddle such and call it preaching the gospel?

The teaching of Jesus Christ is a further manifestation of the power of God the Father Almighty. No man ever taught as he taught, because he received his teaching directly from his Father in heaven. Therefore, he boldly declares that "the law and the prophets were until John." In the sharpest conceivable way he distinguishes his teaching

[3] The clearest Christ figure in T. S. Eliot's *The Cocktail Party* is a kind of psychiatric religious seer.

from the teaching of the venerable traditions so dear to the hearts of his hearers. In the place of these traditions a new law, a new righteousness (the law and righteousness of the Kingdom itself), are given. A new covenant is now in force.

The power of God is in Jesus Christ when he forgives sins. No merely human agent could exercise this authority in his own right; and, therefore, when Jesus Christ explicitly forgives sins, he also explicitly declares that he does so as the agent of the kingdom of God. His authority is that of the Messiah, Son of man (Mark 2:10).

Jesus Christ wields this divine power in the interests of something greater than harmonious social relationships. He works to reveal at once the true character and the imminence of the Kingdom. Only through forgiveness and in the spirit of forgiveness is entrance into the Kingdom possible (Matt. 18:15). This forgiveness must be sought immediately, for the Kingdom is very close, and there is no other way to prepare for it. Put away, then, all thought and wish of acquiring through proper conduct and seemly character anything of a head start over other applicants and suppliants for the Kingdom. Beyond repentance, whatever else is necessary in order to endure the manifold afflictions of the present hour at the end of the age, and to work productively until time runs out, the Spirit of the divine community will provide.

It is no inspired social revolutionary—feet on the earth of solid actuality, head in the lovely blue of pure ideality—who proclaims these things. The Lord of the Kingdom, revealed in and to history, proclaims them.

The final and absolutely decisive revelation of God's power is seen in the Resurrection of Jesus Christ from the dead. God's act here sets the seal upon the divine promises concerning the Kingdom, and at the same time it is the ultimate divine testimony in history to the lordship of Christ (cf. Eph. 1:16-23).

OUR LORD, JESUS CHRIST

There can be little doubt that in the New Testament community the Resurrection is the turning point of Christian faith. If Christ be not risen, the new community is illusion and there is no Kingdom to proclaim to the world. A Kingdom in heaven there may yet be; but no Kingdom erupting into our history. But by the power of God, Christ is risen, and God "will judge the world in righteousness by a man whom he has appointed, and of this he has given assurance to all men by raising him from the dead" (Acts 17:31). Whom God has brought forth from the grave, he has now elevated to a position of glory beyond all other beings, a position which is his full and just due.

Reflection upon this elevation of Jesus Christ opens out into the second main line of interpretation of the lordship of Jesus Christ. So, at least, Christian history runs. Is this movement of Christian history continued in us, or are we another chapter in another story? Our attitude toward resurrection very strongly suggests the latter. We inherit from the Christian past at this point a profound disquietude rather than anything we can take unto ourselves as truth. Indeed, disquietude may be a word far too weak to describe adequately our state of mind—we who once fondly believed that resurrection had been decently interred by the undertaking concern called the modern mind, while the element of truth in the ancient superstition had been sublimated into spiritual value. But behold! Resurrection is again risen in the present theological world!

Perhaps some of our uneasiness over resurrection arises out of the groundless fear that the renewal of resurrection faith means turning back the clocks. Perhaps we have visions of the reopening of those musty, dusty courtrooms in which the evidences of the Resurrection were rehearsed and examined endlessly and profitlessly; and we fear that we shall have to listen again to the everlastingly tedious debates on the reliability of witnesses of resurrection, on the state of their world views, on their gullibility, and so forth. Is any or all of this in store for us? No, and thanks be to God for this considerable favor. Resurrection is *actuality* as well as event or act, and therefore we are not thrown back into the past to get at its being and its truth. The Holy Spirit does not commission the church to exhaust itself rummaging about in archives and documents and in all the musty storage bins of corporate memory in order to find resurrection. Rather, the Spirit enjoins the people of the church to lay hold of the concrete actuality around and upon which the ongoing life of the church is woven. This actuality is an ongoing, everlasting community, and that community is solidly rooted in resurrection.

In New Testament faith resurrection is not a fable upon which to hang the hope of immortality—a Jewish substitute for a more rational Greek philosophical attitude. First of all, and above all, resurrection has to do with a community under covenant. By resurrection men are established in a community, and a community established in eternity is disclosed in history. In this community the enemies of life and spirit are overcome and the enjoyment of being in communion with God opens upon plains inexhaustibly fertile, nourished by the river of the water of life. God through resurrection secures for us our inheritance of this community, for it is Jesus Christ, the first-born of many, who is risen.[4]

---

[4] Individualistic enjoyment of the life of eternity is nowhere involved in this picture, because the biblical comprehension of the realities of the human situation and of divine promise and divine act preclude any and all radical individualisms. Persons find ultimate fulfillment in a community which embraces the living and the dead. Therefore, persons "rise into the life of glory," not as egos, in our modern sense, but as participants of community who are nothing apart from community. (Biblical notions of "person" and "community" are extraordinarily formidable for the contemporary mind in this country; and they are clearly entirely beyond those who piously

OUR LORD, JESUS CHRIST

There is another component in our uneasiness about resurrection, and this component is also a groundless fear. We do not want to open the doors of belief to miracle. But, resurrection is not a miracle, if by miracle we mean a divine interruption of the laws of nature or an uncanny suspension of natural patterns of cause and effect. So to look upon the matter is to suppose that the "laws" of nature (better to say the *forces* of nature) are hostile to creative spirit and to personal existence, so far as they conspire to destroy the body. But in New Testament faith it is not nature which threatens our entering into the promises of God. Let us say it again, the threats to human fulfillment are not the forces of nature: these threats are principalities and powers which are bent upon the disruption of community. These are the conspirators against creative spirit and personal existence; these malign agencies are committed to one purpose and one program: disintegration and dissolution of the bonds of fellowship. Their dominion is for mortal spirits a hideous servitude, a terrible living death. God acts in Christ to destroy their malevolent dominion. And when the Kingdom comes in palpable glory and all the secret things of that life are made manifest, the last of these enemies, even death, will be destroyed.[5]

Resurrection is, then, the creation of salvation, the final historical sign that the new community is now in our midst and that Jesus Christ is the Lord of this life. This same Jesus Christ is thus shown forth as the Lord of history. He is God-with-us, incarnate Word, Son of God. This is the movement of Christian history and Christian experience: from the apprehension of Jesus Christ as the supreme witness to the kingdom of God and as that One in whom the

---

invoke the Bible in support of free enterprise, private property, the open market, and in attacks upon the Welfare State.

[5] "The last enemy to be destroyed is death." (I Cor. 15:26.)

power of God did fully dwell, to the apprehension of Jesus Christ as Lord of lords and Son of God.

2. The second major line of interpretation of Jesus Christ is that he is incarnate Word and Son of God.

"Son of God" in the New Testament has no connection with any metaphysical question of Christ's status in the Godhead. "Son of God" there expresses the dignity and authority of messiahship conferred upon Jesus by the Almighty Father because of Jesus' absolute obedience even unto death upon the cross. This obedience is Jesus' full response to his heavenly vocation: God has chosen him to be his Messiah, to be the envoy of the Kingdom.[6] The metaphysical questions come several centuries later in response to specific and important needs; and when they do arise, they do not obliterate or throw into the shadow the powerful testimony of the earliest Christian fellowship, namely, the witness that Jesus is Christ and Son of God because he is so ordained from eternity and because he is supremely obedient to the demands of the kingdom of God. Wherefore he is the first-born among many, that heir through whose marvelous beneficence we may hope to become joint heirs of the power and glory.

"Obedience" is the key word in this affirmation of the New Testament church. It means that the man Jesus is wholly responsive to the call of God. It means also that

---

[6] "And being found in human form he humbled himself and became obedient unto death, even death on a cross. Therefore God has highly exalted him and bestowed on him the name which is above every name, that at the name of Jesus every knee should bow, in heaven and on earth and under the earth, and every tongue confess that Jesus Christ is Lord, to the glory of God the Father." (Phil. 2:8-11.) The "therefore" of the ninth verse does not necessarily mean a logical consequence or a decision to act in a certain way because Jesus has acted in a certain way. It may mean "whereupon," that is, when some part of a prearranged plan has been realized, then the next part of it, also prearranged, is realized. Unfortunately, as I see the matter, the ambiguities of Paul's "therefores" open the door to Augustinian and Calvinist determinisms.

OUR LORD, JESUS CHRIST

there is in, or with, Jesus a divine function which is in some sense subordinate to God the Almighty Father, as a son is subordinate to a father.[7] But the obedience of Christ is more than the obedience of a prophet. His is the obedience of the Son who enjoys the utmost intimate communion with the Father. "I and the Father are one." (John 10:30.) What Christ says and does, he does and says as the Father instructs (cf. John 8:28). Thus the obedience of Christ reveals a participation in the life of Deity qualitatively and essentially dissimilar to anything men could claim for themselves. Jesus Christ alone participates fully in the will and work of the Almighty Father. "Christ," then, is not really a term suggesting great dignity and distinction in the human world; it is rather, a term for Deity. What is creaturely can never become God; only God is God. Therefore, since Jesus Christ is Lord, he is chosen to be such from eternity; and he does not earn the title simply by dint of ultimate devotion to the cause of the Kingdom in history.

To be chosen from eternity—does this not very naturally suggest that God makes a mark upon his calendar to remind himself that he has a plan for time that he must unroll piece by piece, day by day? Does it not suggest the determinate purpose of God in accordance with which Jesus is steered and pushed along in his role, the subject of a destiny over which he exercises not the slightest control?

---

[7] "Subordinate" is a word with unfortunate connections in the history of Christian dogma. It comes trailing odors of heresy and of violent metaphysical controversy. Since the people of the contemporary church are probably not sensitive to these odors, or at any rate will have trouble identifying them, I venture to use the term simply to suggest that Jesus Christ in his earthly ministry points steadily beyond himself to God the Transcendent Father and that he points with a power and a purity that place him far, far beyond the prophets in Israel. A prophet he "and more than a prophet."

(cf. Acts 2:23). We cannot deny that the New Testament provides grist for the mills of theological and metaphysical determinisms which bind even Jesus Christ the Son of God to the fateful decrees of God the Transcendent. It is enough here to understand the resultant of those systems: they cannot cope with God the Revealer, who, as such, establishes *mutuality in love as his will and as the ultimate situation of and for all being.* If, then, we extricate ourselves from these metaphysical perspectives, we shall see that the New Testament witness to Jesus Christ is that he creates his destiny through his personal decision in freedom. The creative Word is fully present in him and delivers him over only to what he wills. Jesus is the Christ; and the Christ is the creative and redemptive Word of God, that utterance of the Father, that going forth in freedom, by which the worlds spring into being and in which the whole creation finds its blessed fulfillment (cf. Col. 1:16; John 1:3).

The church confesses that Jesus Christ is incarnate Lord because this Word dwelt fully in Him. There the Word became flesh and dwelt among us full of his grace and truth; and "we have beheld his glory, glory as of the only Son from the Father" (John 1:14). He is the Lord of the Kingdom, and of his dominion there is no end. His dominion is history as well as eternity. Accordingly when he says, "My kingdom is not of this world," he does not mean that he is abdicating the lordship of history or postponing his coming in power. The kingdom of God is not a worldly kingdom. It is not the kind of community human enterprise can create and sustain, though to the noblest and clearest spirits in all ages and among all peoples it is given to dream of it. The Kingdom is essentially different from the world; but it is in the world and it has overcome the world. It is in the world because Jesus Christ brought it; and it overcomes the world through Christ's continuous presence in the world.

OUR LORD, JESUS CHRIST

3. So we are brought to the third primary line of interpretation of the lordship of Jesus Christ: Jesus Christ *is* the kingdom of God.

Ordinarily we do not use a person's name to designate or describe a particular kind of community.[8] Yet this is just what happens when the people of the New Testament come to grips with the actualities of God's revelation. The community revealed and created in history through Jesus the Lord is "Christ." To be caught up in the re-creative life of this community is to be in Christ; and to be in such a community is to be a new creature.

As we shall see in some detail in Chapter V, this new community is a great deal more than a memorial or commemorative society, that is, a society built around the memory of an heroic and beloved leader. The power and the life of the community is God-with-us-always, even the Holy Spirit. The Spirit is the presiding and pervading holy Presence who makes known directly the things of God. In John's terms this Presence is the Counselor sent by the Lord to minister to the community when he himself has departed to be with the Father. Here again we see the closest kind of mutuality in Deity revealed, now between Christ Jesus and the Spirit.

The other primary lines of interpretation of the lordship of Jesus Christ are taken up into this final one. The power of God in Jesus is the power of the Kingdom now established in history. The invincible love of Jesus is the very bond of unity of the Kingdom. The resurrection Lord is

---

[8] There are exceptions. A person may say to his beloved, "I am all wrapped up in you." If we suppose that he means this seriously, and if we suppose that he is not a fool, we should conclude that the "you" signifies a situation as well as (or even rather than) the other individual ego. The situation pronounced all-embracing and all-important is one of mutuality in love; and he pays the beloved a compliment genuinely metaphysical when he says that the situation is better named after her than after himself.

the Life of the Kingdom, both in history and in eternity.

We have been holding up to ourselves the church's primary historical witness to God in Christ. The "story to tell to the nations" is that God is in Christ reconciling a sinful world unto himself. This is the gospel that the church is commissioned to preach to the entire world. From the beginning the people of the church have said: Here in Jesus Christ God is acting for all mankind. All mankind must hear these tidings, not only because the secret is too great to be kept a secret, but also because others have the right and the need to hear it. They too are sheep of God's fold.

Is the heart of the gospel still at the heart of our Christian work in and for the world? We people of the church instinctively answer, "Be it even so, Lord," and we can point to certain facts to confirm the wish: the biblical witness to Jesus Christ is still revered; we are still proud to stand in a discernible historical continuity with the people of the New Testament; we own to a place in the holy catholic Church; we give of our substance (a little less than 2 per cent) to support the work of the church; we are proud to announce that our culture is Christian. Nevertheless, the picture is ambiguous. We have substituted a philosophical world view for historical and concrete actualities. We lend every sanction to the conviction that the heart of God's demand is met and written off in full by the acquisition of moral character—that kind of character we believe to have been most notably exemplified in Jesus of Nazareth. We have made the gospel a blueprint for a just and peaceful social order—"have made" is correct, since more lately we feel that the whole concern of the church for society should go into the defense of our society against the assaults of Communism. We are making the gospel a sedative and a nerve tonic; and we have represented Jesus Christ to our contemporaries as being a charmingly amiable prescription druggist equipped to care for all the surface scratches and itches on our psyches—the deeply wounded victims of our world, we hurry along to the psychiatrist in the inner sanctum of science.

Our situation as modern Christians is ambiguous. What has happened to the apostolic zeal for the Kingdom in this situation? There is a real question. We do not see very clearly how to answer it, but we do see certain things which are involved in an answer. We see that evangelical zeal which does not spring from the humble confession of the absolute lordship of Jesus Christ is certain to be synthetic, shallow, and finally confused and misdirected. Jesus Christ is Lord in the church and over the church. It is Jesus Christ alone who reconciles us with God the Almighty Father, even as it is said, "No man comes to the Father except through the Son." The peace, power, and beauty of the Kingdom are ours only through its Lord, Jesus Christ.

The "story" which the church is appointed to publish concerns God's gracious action in behalf of mankind. So mighty an act richly suggests that a mankind for whom it is performed is without hope or help in and for itself. Accordingly, we turn our attention now to the human situation which God's presence in Christ illuminates and redeems.

IV

The Human Situation

THE MESSAGE WHICH THE CHURCH IS IMPERATIVELY CONstrained to preach concerns the whole and the essential human situation. The gospel is to be preached to mankind as a whole because every person is involved in this essential situation. Souls are to be saved, not to make the heap of the redeemed as high, and otherwise as impressive, as possible; but because every soul participates both in a fate and in a promise inherent in human life. If a person rightly apprehends this situation, he will seek deliverance from the fate, and he will hope for fulfillment of the promise. The gospel is the essential clue to the right apprehension of the human situation. And the Lord revealed by it is God, working deliverance and promising fulfillment.

Before going further let us note that we are not at all committed to the hopeless task of getting everything we need to know about mankind out of the Bible, as though it were an encyclopedia containing all significant information about human life. Encyclopedic information is not what we need. We need clues that will point us steadily towards the concrete actualites, and we need courage to grasp the actualities for what they really are. "Clues" there are in the Scriptures; but they come to effective life only in a community. So also for the requisite courage to acknowledge the actualities; only a community can generate and sustain this kind of courage. As Christians we profess to believe that we live and move and have our being in a community which provides illumination and courage adequate for comprehension and acceptance of the human situation.

Christian faith relates us to the actualities of the human situation. These actualities are: creation, guilt, and redemption.

1. We begin with the actualities of creation, the recognition that we are created to be persons. We then recognize that to be a person means to have being in four contexts or essential conditions: the context of nature, the context of society, the context of community, the context of history.[1]

These contexts or conditions of being are not phases which succeed one another in time as we grow into personhood. They define, or help to define, the essential structure of personal existence.

Human existence is set in the context of nature. In this context man apprehends himself as *spirit*. In biblical terms, man is at once an earthly creature among other earthly creatures, and he is the lord and master of all other earthly creatures (Gen. 1:26). Man is created with powers that the other creatures of dust do not have. The Old Testament does not explicitly identify these powers, but so far as man's response to God the Almighty Father is represented as being essentially different from anything other

---

[1] In classical philosophy and theology the term used for the enquiry into the fundamental structures and modes of being was "ontological." After long neglect (except in Roman Catholic circles), the term is again in respectable currency (except in the philosophical circles where men have no appetite for the problems of being). In contemporary thought, however, there is a significant variety in the employment of the term "ontological": on the one hand, there are those who use it to designate something like the classical enquiry suggested above, but, on the other hand, there are those who use it to designate an enquiry into the structures and modes of human being rather than being in general and as such. Since I do not intend to use the term systematically in this discussion, it hardly matters which of these usages is to be preferred to the other.

earthly creatures are capable of, the powers are certainly implied. *These are the powers of spirit.*

The word "spirit" in this context does not mean a kind of substance essentially different from another kind of substance called "matter." [2] "Spirit" is that by which man, a child of nature, is able to transcend nature. This transcendence of nature is a far richer condition and power than what the modern world means by "mastery of nature." For the modern mind, nature is commonly understood as the realm of the purely physical or material. Once upon a time, the physical was thought to be purely inert and passive; and then the work of spirit was to mold it and motivate it and make of it what spirit designed and desired. But the modern mind no longer so conceives it. The physical is in motion—constant, unoriginated, and purposeless motion. An important change in the concept of spirit attends this change in the concept of matter. "Spirit" is either a whispy, filmy excrescence magically thrown up and off by "hurrying stuff"; or it is a being independent of the physical yet able to impose its will upon matter, which, for all of that benign interference, persists in unqualified and unbroken obedience to the "laws of nature"! (Modern man's distaste for miracles of ancient narrative can easily be explained therefore: he is unable to keep pace with the daily demands to make room for new, up-to-date miracles!)

Man's actual transcendence of nature is not at all adequately grasped by the image of a shrewd mechanic presiding over a dumb machine (to say nothing of the converse image, so dear to the heart of materialists: an unwittingly shrewd machine presiding over its spawn, the dumb mechanics). For one thing, we have no concrete basis for

---

[2] The Bible does not go in for these metaphysical distinctions. Christian thought eventually was—and is yet—compelled to pay very serious attention to distinctions of this sort, but the Bible does not begin with them.

emptying everything out of nature and leaving only the "brute physical." Nature pulses with life. (Children and artists until they are corrupted by bad philosophy know this; and if your educated adult—resembling nothing so much as a kernel of rice with all roughness of individuality and nutriment carefully burnished away—knows it not, then let him turn and go to school to children and uncorrupted artists.) For another thing, human life is caught up in a pattern of mutuality with the life of nature. Between us and nature there is give and take. We cannot by simple fiat impose our wills upon nature—I cannot say to nerve or muscle cell: "Servant, go thou quickly and do so and so," with any reasonable hope of obedient response. But when my being as a whole has come to a decision, nerve and muscle cell leap smartly to their ordained tasks; and dreams are realized; and aspirations, some noble, some mean, bend the powers of being and the "laws of nature" to compliance.

But the powers of spirit run beyond these patterns of mutuality. Spirit is essentially creative; and spirit's greatest achievements are at once the glories of civilization and the fulfillment of nature. And, again, for whatever reasons, children and creative artists seem best able to acknowledge this without capitulation to grandiosity and provincialism. The child crouches by the sea and builds a city in the sand with a solemnity that plainly says, "All the waters of all the seas, and all the sands of their far-flung shores, have no other final purpose than to submit to the work of my hands." What does it matter that the tides will dissolve his creation? He will build again and then again; and each creation will wholly justify the whole existence of sand and sky and water. What does it matter that the tides will claim each fresh creation? Other children on other shores will do what he has done, as long as the tides and the seasons run. (There are far graver things to contemplate than the ruination of his empires in the sand: the child will become a man, and he will put away the laughter and the tears of creation, and he will be compelled to make a good living, and to covet success, and to use the last shred of creative spirit in "entertainment" or "amusement" or "having fun" or "getting religion." In all of which to find a moment's respite from the tedium and the pure horror of it all.)

Or consider the artist—poet, painter, or whatever. His work is no more superfluity, so far as nature is concerned. It does not matter whether the nightingale attends when the poet sings: "Thou wast not born for death, immortal Bird!" What matters is that something of nature takes on a novel richness from the poet's free, creative spirit. And this is the artist's intent, as artist. If people are amused, edified, horrified, titillated, bewildered, or bewitched by what he has done, well, they are probably feeling conformable to convention and not conformable to concrete actuality. To be sure, the artist would communicate: the creation *is* his communication. As a rule he cannot be held responsible for the program notes. These little aids for the digestion of the culture consumers have nothing to do with the artist's creative activity. They are written to stand between creative spirit and decently civilized people—they are the screen around the delivery-room table. Thus we are told that in the *Pathétique* we can hear the cries of Tchaikovsky suffering the pangs of unrequited love, cries now muted and acquiescent, now hoarse and defiant. But, the cries of the artist are *not* the cries of a jilted or a jaded lover: there is a profound, a qualitative difference between them. The sufferings of love may inspire a poem, a symphony, or a wood carving. But when an artist lays hold of this suffering, a novel richness infuses it. When he shows this suffering to us, it is not a photographic or phonographic imitation of something once experienced before. From his creation you could never hope to find out what his love affair had really been.

Moreover, the artist is not obliged as artist to duplicate or imitate nature. Merely clever people can do this, with a comic perfection that sends us scurrying off into closets and attics and antique shops of memory to see whether the "cover artist" has depicted Grandmother's coffee mill as faithfully as we think he has. The photographic and therefore the comic perfection of the portraits we see on our magazine covers shows true humanity cunningly concealed beneath the sentimentalities of our culture. The realities of human life in the context of nature are forgotten until a courageous and creative spirit decides that he will paint the arthritic hand as he sees it; and then the story of that hand emerges as an anguished contention of spirit with nature and perchance with God; and as the painter tells that story, he refuses to expurgate any part of it in order to make it come out right. He is not interested in comic perfection of detail: he is interested in the truth; and the truth can be grasped and expressed only in and through the pangs of creation.

In the context of nature, then, the human situation exhibits the creative powers of spirit.

Human existence is set in the context of society. In this context man apprehends himself as ego, the individual self.

Comprehension of this actuality has been sadly confused by bad philosophy and by theology far too uncritical of its dependence upon this philosophy. The creed generally identified as "individualism" is a triumph of this confusion. In this creed we see a stubborn denial of the most obvious, the most palpable of facts, namely, that the "self" is a creature of society. Pursue this creature into the inmost caverns of privacy and solitude, and you will hear that interior welkin ring with the cries of the human pack. Unravel the tangled web of all his dreams and of all his visions, and you will find fragments and oddments—queerly blended and joined, no doubt—of a world he never made but which made him.

An ego is a self-differentiation[3] of a condition of being we call "society." It is also true that society (in the strictly human sense) is a state of affairs defined by ego and alter ego. There are no other essential ingredients of society than selves. Nature figures in society so far only as an object and a realm of human concerns. Society is the distinctively human world.

This structure of ego and other ego is a created actuality. It is a fact confirmed by the social sciences but not established as fact by the social sciences. It is rock-bottom fact; and as such, we cannot escape it or modify it. When we speak of the impersonality of society, we are calling attention to this fact. Society is always threatening to reduce this ego or that ego to the status of a mere unit, as, for example, for the purposes of a military campaign or for calculation of a wage increase or decrease. This reduction means that real and important differences among the units are neglected or obliterated. This loss is not always felt to be a misfortune. Indeed, the anonymity of being a mere unit sometimes becomes exquisitely attractive to an ego penalized one way or another for its distinctiveness.

In the context of society human creatures are bound to one another whether or not they will to be so bound. An individual can, upon occasion, will to dissolve his connections with certain other individuals. This project is sometimes crowned with success, provided that the bonds are relatively superficial and attenuated, for example, those of a business partnership. Proposals to throw off more funda-

---

[3] A self-differentiation which at once both presupposes and realizes "selves." Selves are the differentiated units by which a society is constituted. A society is the interaction of these differentiated units. This is the situation in which persons come to self-awareness, and in which many critical decisions have to be made along the route to freedom.

mental bonds meet with indifferent success, where they are not overwhelmingly rejected, not by the specific resolutions of other individuals, but by an inarticulate, unconscious, and massive consensus.

Nature and the universe as realms of inflexible law are projections of the effective image of society. A norm or law is essentially a social concept: it suggests that peculiar combination of what-must-be and appeal to a human mind and will to acknowledge it so. A natural fact, on the other hand, is just what it is: we are not obliged to acknowledge it in any significant sense of the word. But a norm is a social fact in the sense suggested. *It demands acknowledgment, in the peculiar sense that without this acknowledgment it has no force and no reality whatever.* It may survive my disinclination to acknowledge it. But let it slip, unnoticed or spurned, out of the context of acknowledgment, and it survives henceforth only as a pallid ghost, of interest only to the historian who cannot distinguish one order of fact from another.

The third actual context of the human situation is community. In this context man apprehends himself as *love*. A person is more than an individual ego, because unique and essential potentialities are exploited by community that are only incidentally called into play by either society or nature. This is not so much a matter of unique faculties as it is of a unique expression of native potentialities.

Thus imagination operates at all levels of human life. In the realm of *community* it has a unique function: by imagination the person puts himself in the place of other members of the community. He participates in their situations, indeed, in their lives. By imagination he not only envisages and projects ideal aims, he also judges the adequacy or inadequacy of these aims by anticipating the effects of their pursuit and realization. This act of judgment is "feeling the feelings" of others, and its ordinary name is sympathy.

Love is more than sympathy, but sympathy is one of its essential components. Another of these essential components is the will. By "will" we understand that power of concrete resolution of the person whereby he projects himself in one direction rather than another. When he loves, he projects himself toward another, whose situation he penetrates sympathetically. He resolves *to be* for this other. He pledges himself to the other.

Love is a situation of genuine mutuality, that is, one in which two (or more) persons resolve *to be* for each other. Only in this kind of situation is there fulfillment of personal being. To be a person means to be in a situation of genuine mutuality—or, at the very least, to be moving or working toward such a situation.

Now we ought not suppose that community is a mere ideal, forever unrealized but forever alluring. Community is an actual structure of personal existence, just as love is an actual power. We are made in and for community—this is laid down in the plan of creation. These actualities are susceptible of corruption. The corruption of the nonactual (if that suggests anything at all) is a mere trifle compared with the degradation of actual structures and the misdirection and dissipation of actual powers of being.

Let us note also that community is not an excrescence upon society, a late-comer upon a stage already set and dominated by shrewder actors with stronger voices. Presently we shall have to see that community is the foundation of society, and that love is the actual cohesive force in all human association.

The fourth actual context of the human situation is history. In this context man apprehends that the meaning of his life is determined in and by the past. The context of history is the realm of fate or destiny because here men see

THE HUMAN SITUATION

themselves (as individuals or as a temporal cross section of a people or culture) acting out a part already and long since assigned them. We can make choices: but only such choices as conform to our destiny. This is the primary pattern of historical judgment, and every serious and productive effort to determine what the past was, to determine, that is, what is historical fact, is an effort descended from this primary pattern of historical judgment and is related to it as content is related to form. When moreover, epic poets, seers, and prophets people their decisive past with heroes and saints, golden surely and perhaps divine, we must not lose sight of their serious intent: to disclose deeper and darker aspects of history. "Look," they say, "from this noble breed we are derived. We are the seed of their greatness and their glory. If all had gone well, we too should have walked the earth proudly and justly, as befits the sons and daughters of the gods. But all has not gone well! The gold is corrupted with base alloy. Our pride is sickness; and our justice is mockery. But where is the blame? Our history is to be blamed, but we are all the guilty ones, we and our fathers before us, and our children after us."

Thus history is shown forth as fate but as more than fate. *History is what man has done to himself.* History is the bond—stronger than iron, more impalpable than flesh—which links man present to man past and man future.[4]

Here the Bible is our great schoolmaster. The biblical teachers never let us lose sight of the real significance of history. *Their symbols are taken from the dramatic encounters of persons with persons.* Human life is not portrayed as but one expression of nature's rhythms or as one

[4] Nothing is more natural than that we should use symbols of flesh and of nature to express historical determination and historical connection. But symbols they remain, and unless we are schooled to note the difference between the symbol and the reality symbolized, the uniqueness of the realm of history vanishes from our sight.

effect of nature's laws. The movement of the human spirit is not bound to or by the movements of the heavenly bodies. Therefore, no one can plumb the mystery of the future. Except God disclose it, it is dumb to our every question, but not as nature is dumb. Things are being shaped and prefigured in God, who rules the future absolutely. It is he who is relentless, not our stars. If our fathers' folly and our own is bound to us, God is the one who drove the rivets! God is the Creator: God is the Judge.

2. We have been reflecting upon the actualities of creation. To be a person is to have existence in the created realms of nature, society, and history. But beyond the actualities of creation there are also the actualities of guilt and its consequences. Here we must deal with sin, degradation, and damnation.

Guilt pertains to the human situation as such. Sin is the individual person's appropriation and acknowledgment of this guilt. In everyday conversation we reverse the relation of guilt to sin and say that a person is guilty for his sin or his sins. In reality, however, guilt stands for something much wider and deeper than this ordinary usage would ever lead us to imagine. The wider and deeper actualities are notoriously difficult to delineate prosaically and systematically. Efforts along this line have occasioned great and grim theological battles, the renewal of which is not to be entered upon lightheartedly. But the weight of the gospel compels us to grasp the actualities of our situation for what they are and for this purpose to think of ourselves whatever must be thought. Thus we are led to invert the relation of sin and guilt, not, to be sure, to the place where we say we sin because we are guilty. Nevertheless, we sin in the context of guilt. Guilt is not the cause of our sin, but neither did that guilt spring into existence with that sin.

Guilt, so understood, is at once the word for a situation and for awareness of that situation. The situation is that of an existence violently wrenched away from its proper destiny; the awareness is powerfully compounded of flaring rebellion and of shamed dejection. It is in this situation and in this awareness of our situation that we sin.

Accordingly, what we are to understand by "sin" is something rather more than a conscious and voluntary violation of a moral law. Violation of "moral law" so far does not adequately indicate that sin is a violation of fundamentally personal relationships. Sin is an offense against an essentially personal order of affairs. *The offense precisely is the will to treat persons as less than persons; and, therefore, sin is a rebellion against the actualities of creation.*

In relation to the realm of spirit, sin is the will to deny the uniquely creative powers of personal existence by submerging these powers under nature. Here are the sins of sensuality, of brutishness and beastliness, and of all that smacks of a sick longing to be as the animals. The fulfillment of all such aspirations itself calls for some outlay of creative imagination, even though the desired end state is oblivion as much as it is animal ecstasy or placidity. Proper animals, on the other hand, are not afflicted with aspirations; they live uncreatively and are herewith content.[5] What a piteous thing it is, therefore, for a man to employ his unique resources to become less than a man! Piteous it is because foredoomed to failure: the sinner, in the realm of spirit, is neither a successful man nor a successful animal!

In relation to the realm of society (the order of ego and other ego) sin is the will to make the other-self an adjunct of one's own self. Egoism is the customary title for this policy. It is a policy which has many degrees of clarity and comprehensiveness. At one end of the scale there is the

[5] A psychologist may capture some of these proper animals and spend his career in discovering how to make them neurotic. This is called "the Advancement of Science."

natural selfishness of the child; at the other, the wild disease of egomania. Somewhere along the line in between there is the philosopher's pet, the cool moment of calculation in which one seeks that maximum gain for self which entails minimum loss for others. Child, egomaniac, and man of reason—all own a common core: the will to make ego the capital of the world. This is sin because it violates the created order.

In relation to the order of personal existence sin is violation of love. Here sin really comes into its own. Sensualism and egocentricity are indeed corruptions of creation, but they do not contain in themselves the key to the riddle; they point beyond themselves, as symptoms point to a deeper malignancy. That deeper malignancy is lovelessness, or to put it in more dynamic terms, repudiation of love.

Repudiation (rejection) of love purposefully omits nothing from its violence. Ego is not exempted from its fury, nor the flesh. Lovelessness is beyond egoism just as surely as it is beyond altruism. It is beyond sensuality just as surely as it is beyond spirituality. The rebel has no prepared defense to fall back upon except—hatred. There is no sanctuary from the roaring plague except—the pesthouse!

Here guilt comes into its own. Here we see it revealing something far more significant than bad conscience or self-accusation for not having fulfilled society's expectations. For suppose we ask this most wretched of all God's creatures (forgetting not even for a minute that he is Everyman) what accounts for his situation. What will he reply? Everything and nothing, he will answer. Everything: God wounded him in eternity, his mother scalded him while yet in her womb with the vitriol of rejection, society is a hateful conspiracy against him, and so on. Nothing: there is no explanation save existence itself. To be is to be unloved; to be unloved is to be unloving; and there is an end to it.

THE HUMAN SITUATION

Querulous or not, this is nonetheless a true bill drawn against existence. Specifically, it is an indictment against existence as history. History is the grand worker of deadly mischief, for while it does not make me choose what I choose, it establishes the context of all my choices. The world I never made is the world of history. I can defy other worlds, whether nature or heaven. Fate I can engage in no satisfying quarrel. Hence, since I cannot get at the real enemy, I strike at substitutes, venting upon them an anger and a hatred enormously inflated and inflamed by futility. If, therefore, I treat others as the pawns and playthings of my fancy, now benign and now cruel but neither from inclusive resolution, it is because I sense myself a plaything of history, a bastard offspring of chance and necessity; and who doubts but that bastards come into the world with a magnificent endowment—of hatred?

Everyman here bespeaks the actualities of damnation. For the purposes of a certain limited piety, damnation can be represented as the condition of being under juridical condemnation, but ultimately this representation will not do at all. Juridical condemnation is at best an outward form, fashioned arbitrarily even in the best of human societies. Its extension to God and the divine Kingdom but serves to reveal in devastating clarity how external and arbitrary this form is. The actualities of damnation elude apprehension through so defective a symbol. It is far more adequate to think of damnation as a condition of irremediable alienation and isolation from community for one's own decisions. To be damned is to carry a burden of guilt out of all proportion to one's powers. So to be exiled from the land of the living, and so to be burdened is to be in hell. Thus, to be damned is to live in hell—that actual condition in which the true good is no longer good for us because we have lost any real power to pursue and to attain it. Wherefore we profess to find it desirable to be—in hell.

Degradation is also a part of the human situation. To be degraded is not only to feel cheapened and dirtied, it is also to endure a real diminution of power and the crippling of potentialities. Society can easily convince us that to do certain things is "dirty," and it can demonstrate that dirty people are penalized, and that the really filthy ones are banished. But again the realities of degradation run far beyond the realities of society's "dirt." (For that matter, real degradation is sometimes extravagantly rewarded by a society.)

Loss of the power of being is damnation only when it is a product of settled policy, that is, *when it is something willed*. In our society persons are made to feel degradation through sheer accident of birth, or through the mere advance of old age and penury. None of these is damnation. Each of them illustrates concretely what it means to be the victim of a settled policy of depersonalization. The victims of such policies are precisely those who are defrauded of truly and fully personal existence.

3. One of the conditions of human existence is, then, guilt, which includes sin, damnation, degradation. To be human is to live in relation to these actualities. What the church is chartered to preach is also related to these actualities.

The mission of the church is to proclaim the message of salvation in Jesus Christ. What the church preaches is the actuality of redemption, which embraces all of man and includes the present moment. This is a very difficult aspect of the church's message and work, because the temptation is ever present to identify some good-intentioned program of societal or private improvement or reconstruction with the whole actuality of redemption. One of the more subtle forms of this temptation is this: a particular kind of behavior is held up by the church as precisely the sort of thing the redeemed man engages in. From this it is all too easy to conclude that anybody is redeemed who honors that kind of behavior. A communion of self-appointed saints then appears, conceived in self-righteousness and dedicated to the oversimplification of the human situation. But, on the other hand, people may become so wary of these temptations that they see redemption as an actual condition postponed to a remote future, or banished altogether from the realm of history. Our ears, when they are closed by this mood, are barren ground for our Lord's word: "This day is salvation come to this house!"

In the evangelical task the church has a continuing and inescapable problem on its hands. The redemption it preaches and shows forth is incomparably greater than our hopes for improvement. And yet every such hope, nobly conceived and wisely wrought, is embraced by this divine actuality of redemption. Not only embraced. Also, and above all else, *transfigured* by this divine actuality, because redemption is the transfiguration of the whole of personal existence. Redemption is an overcoming, but since it is from God, it is not a cancellation of any positive aspect of our creaturely existence. God's redeeming action embraces and transforms all the fundamental structures of personal existence. Let us consider in briefest sketch how this is so:

Redemption means that our eyes are opened upon the concrete possibilities of the overcoming of self. God in Christ delivers us into freedom in and for the world. The horizons of being and of good are no longer bounded by the ego. The world becomes open country; and we are invited to go in and out and find pasture. We are free to live with others and for others. The world is no longer a desert. Lo, it blossoms as the rose.

Redemption means that our eyes are opened upon the concrete possibilities for the overcoming of the world. Jesus Christ delivers us into freedom from the world. Just as we are empowered, from beyond ourselves, to respond affirmatively to the solicitations and demands of the world, we are also empowered to evaluate these solicitations and demands from a perspective transcending the tension between ego and world. The world is not my master, in love or in fear and hate. The world is not my slave, the thing of my desiring. It is not I who have overcome the world—when I essay this, I reduce it to subjection; I cancel this or that aspect of it. Salvation comes to my house when I hear the Lord saying: "Behold, I have overcome the world!" and therefore also when I look about to see the ways in which I am able now to live beyond the tension between ego and world.

The ultimate transfiguration of personal existence occurs at the point of our relation to history. Here redemption means that our eyes are opened upon the concrete possibilities for the overcoming of time and fate. Guilt is dissolved because it is a negativity, and as such it withers and dies in the presence of the Lord of our redemption.

Resurrection and eternal life are the terms most familiar to us in which the ultimate actuality of redemption is suggested. Resurrection signifies a life in which the powers of dissolution have been cancelled. So far as time is a symbol for these powers of dissolution, redemption means that it is overcome. So far, on the other hand, as time is a symbol of creative advance, it is taken up into eternity. Redemption is a present actuality for us just so far as here and now we are empowered to live and to hope beyond the time of anxiety, and just so far as we are able concretely to envisage our historical destinies as wrought in and through freedom rather than by fate.

God's redeeming work is the work of an essential and radical transformation of our existence. The ax of divine judgment in this process is laid only against that which is essentially destructive and corrupting. History, and the career of every person, is full of things accidentally destructive. Everyman's life is a story of the realization of certain possibilities at the cost of other possibilities, and is thus a story compact of regret. The exclusion of what is not compatible with settled and positive purpose argues neither baseness in what is so treated, nor ill will nor ignorance in him who so decides. It argues, rather, finitude, for which condition it is unseemly to feign repentance. The wrath of God is not visited upon this limitation of being that we call finitude, but upon whatever there is that battens upon the degradation of us creatures. If there is anything of which we can soberly say, "Its very existence is an impoverishment of being," then that, and only that, is God's enemy. But are even these demons, these principalities and powers, excluded from redemption?

V

The Holy Spirit and the Church

THE CHURCH IS TO PREACH JESUS CHRIST, WHO SUMMONS all men to participate in the freedom and power of the kingdom of God. The people of the church work in behalf of a community and are sustained by a community in which the possibilities of human existence are affirmed absolutely. The Kingdom the church is commissioned to proclaim is the Kingdom of divine love, eternally and everlastingly pledged to the redemption of the world. Jesus Christ is the foundation and cornerstone of that community. The Holy Spirit is its life. From these affirmations very important consequences flow.

Since Jesus Christ is the foundation of the divine community in history, its bond of unity is divine love. This love is actual, creative, free, and invincible. When we say it is actual, we are pointing to something incomparably more significant than an ethical ideal. We point to a concrete and efficacious power. Ideals are the creations and projections of our minds. Concretely effective powers are ponderable factors in a world that is not the creation and projection of our minds. When we say, secondly, that Christ's love is creative, we mean that it provides inexhaustible possibilities both for the transformation of the old and the injection of real novelty into the world. Thirdly, the freedom of love in Christ is precisely the divine freedom.

THE HOLY SPIRIT AND THE CHURCH

> Immortal Love, forever full,
> Forever flowing free,
> Forever shared, forever whole,
> A never-ebbing sea![1]

Love, as being itself, is bestowed upon us by God the Almighty Father through Jesus Christ his only Son our Lord. We are accustomed to thinking of this affirmation as the great thesis of the Reformation. It is that, but it is also at the very heart of the Christian faith in all ages.[2] In Christ love goes forth ignoring and overcoming all conventional barriers erected between good men and wicked men: "Behold, he eats with sinners and publicans!" The love of God in Christ Jesus overcomes all cultural barriers erected to divide the elect from the expendables. And when this power grasps a man, he declares, "I am debtor to Jew and Gentile"; and, "There is no longer Jew or Gentile." Again, what Jesus Christ does out of love for us sinners, he does not because he is driven by some mastering fate, but because of freely accepted responsibility for the children of God. And just as he moves freely through the walls which divide men from one another, so he moves freely toward the fulfillment of his saving purpose. He draws his destiny upon himself; it is not a magnet irresistibly drawing him to itself.

Fourthly, Christ's love is invincible. In Gospel narratives the demons cower before him and throw themselves upon his clemency. In the witness of the Epistles, he bursts the bonds of death and renders captivity captive. He stands at

---

[1] "Our Master," John Greenleaf Whittier.

[2] In contemporary theology a great deal of attention has been given to the doctrine of divine love, by Catholic as well as by Protestant thinkers. This is one of the few places where the interchange between Catholic and Protestant theologians has been both temperate in tone and genuinely productive. It is hard to conceive that any Christian theme could more richly deserve this kind of treatment!

the door and knocks, "panoplied with nought save perfect love" and the gates of hell cannot prevail against him.

The invincible power of God's love in Christ—how little used we are nowadays to confessing this otherwise than in eighteenth-century hymns which everybody knows by heart but not in the heart. We modern Christians long ago became intrigued by the picture of Jesus the Patient Sufferer. We have remained at the foot of the cross long, long after Christ is laid in the tomb and has come forth. We have preached the utter impotency of divine love in this world, and have vaunted ourselves as archrealists by proclaiming in season and out of season that the world rewards ultimate love with the cross. Does, then, the world yet belong to principalities and powers? Did not Jesus Christ shake their suzerainty to its nethermost foundations? The original commission of the Christian church was to proclaim Christ the victor, not Christ the vanquished. In our time the holy scripture instructs us to lay fresh hold of this commission, the charter of salvation.

The church, then, is grounded in the redeeming love of God in Christ. The Holy Spirit is the life of this community. This life is nothing creaturely or transient, finite or mortal. It is the Holy Spirit, the continuing presence of the Lord in our midst, by which we are sustained in faith, hope, and love; and by which also we are made participants in the actualities of redemption.

The gifts of the Holy Spirit—faith, hope, and love—are ours only in the context of community. They are not for private enjoyment but for enhancement of the common life. ("I had rather speak five words with my understanding.") They are not ours for private edification or aggrandizement, but for the enlargement of the shared life and for the amplification of all its powers. God has so created us that no man lives unto himself alone. Social existence, we have seen, is neither a blind nor a calculated coming together of souls essentially complete apart from society. Personal existence is social by constitution. Hence, the Holy Spirit is the life of a community, not a spark or a flash of private and ineffable inspiration. If we are seized by it in solitude, it is to make clearer and dearer to us the fellowship begun in earth and consummated in heaven.

The work of the Holy Spirit runs beyond this. The gospel of our Lord Jesus Christ is preached only under the inspiration of the Holy Spirit. We are but little tempted to think of this inspiration in terms of the gift of tongues and of other ecstatic phenomena. We are more strongly inclined to feel that the gospel can be adequately proclaimed only by those who feel inspired or exalted. Such feelings are frequently a one-way ticket into bathos and banality, into stale histrionics and wearisome self-dramatization. The Holy Spirit does not attest itself by such feelings and their effects. The inspiration of the Holy Spirit, without which we are clanging cymbals indeed, is Christ's love, by which we are led to bear witness to the power and the peace and the beauty of a Kingdom we have yet to behold with the eyes of the flesh, but whose actuality has grasped us, never to let us go again. The Holy Spirit sanctifies us when the "love of the brethren" constrains us to the sacrifice of self; but this it does only when the brethren are any and all of the children of God. God in the Spirit does not sanctify the discriminations and preferential arrangements of the world. And so far as our love is bounded by these, it is not holy but profane, and all the usages of piety will not make it otherwise.

Truly, only the Spirit can sanctify the labors and the prayers of the people of the church. We labor and pray productively only where others are able to catch the pulse of the holy community with its blessed promises of forgiveness and of new life.

The Christian life is a corporate, organic enterprise. The church is the body, the manifest form taken upon itself by the Christian life. The church is the fellowship of those who honor Christ as Lord and are sustained in a new being by the Holy Spirit. But the church as we now know it is a much more complex affair than this. The complexities are various and arise from many different quarters. For one thing, the career of the fellowship is complicated by one simple but wholly inevitable fact: *it is comprised of sinful human beings.* The church is not a company of men made perfect, but of men sustained and unified by the promise and hope of perfection.

The life of the church is complicated also by its involvement with the culture around it. It is an institution among other institutions. Its adherents feel, therefore, that it must compete with contemporary institutions for the loyalty of its members and for the loyalty of those whom it would attract to itself. For these purposes the church must offer a digestible justification for its existence and its demands. This is especially true and especially important when the environing culture exhibits and encourages conflicting aims and ideals. In such a situation the people of the church feel a powerful tension: should the aims and ideals of life in the church be set forth as standing in sharp opposition to those of other institutions, or should they be interpreted as complimentary to, if not actually identical with, the aims and ideals of other institutions and of the essential spirit of that culture as a whole? This tension is neither easily resolved nor rendered harmless through long familiarity. In our own day we can see how easy it is for people of the church to feel that the survival of aims and ideals they profoundly believe to be Christian is absolutely dependent upon the survival of the church as they know it. It is apparently easier still to believe that the prospects of high and noble civilization are indissolubly wedded to the prospects of the church and its ideals. If, then, the church is successful in its efforts to increase its power and influence, should not our whole civilization enjoy an elevation and over-all strengthening of its life?

So we are led, by easy stages and without a moment's awareness of conscious descent into ignominious self-righteousness and pride of circumstance and power, into viewing evangelism as a program for obtaining new members of the church and for revitalizing the loyalty of persons already committed to it. We are led to believe that in the church people will profit immeasurably from maximum exposure to the ideal aims of our world, which aims we are certainly prone to impute to the divine moral order itself. And so the church undergoes radical alteration, from the "fellowship of those who honor and obey Christ as Lord and are sustained in a new being by the Holy Spirit," into an institution competing for position and justifying its claim to eminence by citing its sterling contributions to culture and its indispensable role as the depository of high ideals and noble aims.

Caught in this situation we Christians of this age have no real recourse except to pray for that evangel which is the Holy Spirit of truth, who knows immediately the things of God. Surely from that source we may hope to catch a new vision of the church as the evangel of the kingdom of God. But perhaps our hopes should be more moderately expressed. Perhaps we should simply hope again to see and to believe that part of the work of Christian evangelism is to proclaim that the conversion which God demands and provides for is much more than a matter of taking on yet another institutional loyalty. Was there ever a time when this proclamation was so dreadfully important as it now is? See how good men and bad, wise men and foolish, noble men and scoundrels, rally to an ultimate attack upon and an ultimate defense of institutions. Men gird themselves to die for Americanism, a loose name for a highly flexible synthesis of institutions and states of mind; and for Communism, a loose name for dogmas long since both crudely and delicately adulterated by expediential policies. The quality of government is assayed by asking whether it is constitutional, not whether it contributes to human welfare; and blood poured out in faraway places is held a pleasing sacrifice if it gives one day more of life to profits and dividends. Between us and our brethren towering abstractions stalk in a no man's land created by bad philosophy. This is not to say that institutions, social orders and habits, are unreal. Their reality is grounded in the actualities of human will, thought, and feeling, and not in some imagined immutable cosmic scheme. They are, yes; but they are for use; they are made for man.

How pathetically great, then, is the need of the world to hear a really clear and a really truth-dedicated preachment: that creative community runs beyond all our institutions. Let the church, above all, declare that where institutions clash in lethal opposition, human beings may yet hope to compose their differences and out of conflict distill a richer harmony. But the church cannot and will not preach this word unless it is ready, with true, yea, and fiery, evangelical zeal, to point beyond itself to the kingdom of God. In good conscience we people of the church cannot tell others that the radical ills of human life are healed by joining our ranks, or that the ultimate perils of the world are thereby avoided or mollified. But we can say, and we must say, that to join a church may provoke a hunger for a higher righteousness. It may create an awareness of the demand for a world-transcending loyalty, and it may open the eyes for the first time upon the possibilities of communion with God in Christ. We go about seeking those who for these ultimate reasons will identify themselves with those who love Christ and love in him all the sons and daughters of God.

VI

The World and the Kingdom

THE CHURCH IS DEEPLY INVOLVED WITH THE WORLD. CONtrary to scriptural injunction, the church is both in the world and of the world. Yet as the community created in history through Jesus Christ the church is called to show forth the eternal kingdom of God by precept and example. The actual situation of the church is defined by this tension between its divine commission and its worldly involvement.

The people of the church by and large do not seem to be aware of this tension, even though it runs all through the life of the church. Indeed, the church in our time all too often proclaims itself as that great place where all tensions and anxieties are eased and relaxed. But would it not be a blind leader of the blind were it to confess that it, too, lives under powerful tensions? Would not such a confession alienate our contemporaries from the church and leave them with recourse only to medicaments far more mischievous than the mild sedatives now prescribed by the church? This is a real risk, but it must be embraced as such. The church has a mission in the world and a message for the world which are now and will ever be offensive to the world. But it is a matter of the greatest importance that the world should not be offended at the wrong things, or be alienated by something itself alien to the gospel of our Lord Jesus Christ.

What then is the world to which the church is called to proclaim an offending message and for which it is called to lead an offending life? "World" signifies civilization and culture rather than the whole of the created order, or the order of history and of time. A civilization has certain attitudes toward history and time, and these attitudes have always some kind of expression within the church's understanding of itself at any given moment. But, as we shall hope to see, the message of the church contains something that passes judgment upon these attitudes of a civilization toward time and toward itself.

What is the genius, the inner life and drive of civilization? Human creativity, confronted by nature and history. Nature is that from which man must wrest his living (cf. Gen. 3:17-18). Nature is the brute world all-round, which, though it be brute, yet responds to intelligent operation upon it. Man senses in nature mysterious forces, and he apprehends patterns in all its motions and products. And so while men make tools to subdue it, they also attune their hearts to nature's heart, and become poets, artists, mystics, as well as farmers and mechanics. But civilization is also man's response to history. We have always to reckon with the past. Every civilization is a result of a momentous ongoing wrestle of the present with the past. History is therefore a legacy as well as a burden; it bequeaths possibilities, and it constricts potentialities.

A civilization has also to wrestle with competition in the present. It must contend with other civilizations, with, that is, alternative organizations of life and spirit to meet the demands of nature and history. These competitors are sometimes fully developed as such, and sometimes they are more largely undeveloped and implicit; but in either case they are a concrete problem—a threat to the integrity and vitality of a regnant civilization. A flourishing and healthy civilization is able both to identify its competitors as being what they are, and to provide to its own constituents and beneficiaries, at least, a sense of superior value and satisfaction. Yet, even for a healthy civilization there is no permanent or final resolution of this concrete tension, as history fully attests. Sooner or later the once healthy and productive civilization must die a death.

So far we have been dealing with what we may call certain of the natural or plain facts concerning the world or civilization. To these facts the Christian church, from the beginning, has added another not so easily ascertainable: something has gone wrong with the corporate human enterprise called "civilization." Here is something which originally and essentially expresses the will of God, and which now defies the lordship of its creator! In consequence God is now bringing the full weight of his Kingdom to bear upon the world. The world is now under judgment; the kingdom of God bears in upon it relentlessly.

The kingdom of God is in the world for the reproof, chastisement, and condemnation of the world. But he who judges the world is God, whose ways are not our ways and whose thoughts are not our thoughts. He condemns and chastises for the redemption of the world, because his purpose in all things is a creative one. The pressure of the kingdom of God upon and in the world is the pressure of infinite solicitude. The relentlessness of the kingdom of God is the relentlessness of the divine love, which will not relinquish the world to a condign fate.

These are truths expressed in the doctrine of the Incarnation. God's solicitude for the world was so great and all-moving that he sent his Son for its redemption. In the world this Son was fully one of us, "taking the form of a servant," and becoming "sin who knew no sin." And though he was in the world full of the grace and truth of the divine Kingdom, he did not dazzle or overpower us with its glory. "He laid his glory by"; and the Kingdom was among us, humble as the insignificant mustard seed, inconspicuous as the cup of cold water extended to a stranger, and gentle as a good shepherd soothing the terrors and hurts of a storm-battered lamb.

The kingdom of God comes stealthily into the world. It identifies itself with us, becoming breath of our breath and blood of our blood. It comes never in violation of freedom and integrity, for these are its gifts; it is the Kingdom of perfect love.

To stand under the judgment of the kingdom of God is no trivial matter. The people who sit in darkness come to love the darkness. We tremble and shudder when the blazing light of God's noontide breaks in upon us. If love, as Christ reveals it, is the life and law of the divine Kingdom, how shall we fare in and under that Kingdom, we whose hearts are divided to the bottom between love and hate, love and fear? If the principles whereby we determine eminence and preference in our civilization and society are thrown down in the kingdom of God, how shall we fare in it, we whose families, fraternal orders, massive social-political institutions, yes, and churches, are erected around and upon these very principles? Badly, badly, who can doubt it? But the time of faring badly is not postponed. Not by any stretch of the concrete imagination could we suppose that this time is postponed. The church of Christ can promise no invincible sanctuary from tensions and anxieties, because in this church a gospel works, dividing a house against itself, producing a conscience at war with itself, corroding and destroying every false peace and every illusory sense of well-being and security. Judgment upon civilization and upon a church identified with it is not postponed. The kingdom of God is near at hand; it is in our midst.

The divine Kingdom is in the world. It is in the world as an actual community charged with regenerative power. This power is given into the world for the transformation of the

THE WORLD AND THE KINGDOM

world. The church bears witness to this power in itself, as it bears witness to that actual community of which it is the servant and the messenger. In response to this witness people, both in and out of the church, hope for a transformation of civilization, and set mind and hand to specific programs looking in that direction. Too much is expected of these specific programs, and too little; but the hope for a perfect median course is illusory, as the abandonment of all such programs is ungodly despair. God does not summon us to the creation of a perfect social order. He does summon us to the high task of increasing every positive aspect of our common life, and of diminishing everything in it that is destructive and inhuman.

The church is not the kingdom of God. The church is the servant of that Kingdom, and it is often timid and often proud. It is persistently weak, corrupt, and ambiguous; but withal it is a servant through whose stuttering and fearful whispers and through whose vainglorious clamor the gospel gets itself proclaimed! For which thanks be to God alone.

The church is sent to bear witness to the Kingdom in our midst. It also testifies to the Kingdom that is beyond the world and beyond history. The kingdom of God penetrates and permeates the world; but it stands there over against the world, in invincible holiness. Our world is shattered against it, for the Kingdom is established from everlasting to everlasting, and it will not be moved. Our civilization is cracking up, but not because an impersonal law of history so decrees and determines. We drive with a demonic determination upon the shoals. Our world is hounding itself toward a dire end: it is no plaything of fate. We see that the social structures of our world have long since become rigid; or, more accurately stated, our attitude towards these structures is one of unnatural rigidity. To be sure, many of us fancy ourselves as free spirits in respect to moral conventions; but before the massive social structures of our civilization we are much more idolatrous than iconoclastic. Consider what is by now our standard interpretation of the clash between democracy and communism. Each is projected as a self-contained and essentially immutable entity; and it is supposed that between them the possibilities are exhausted; and it is piously held that they are arrayed against each other by a fiat of God. Every proposal looking toward some kind of constructive resolution of the conflict is greeted by howls of "appeasement!" "betrayal!" "softness!" and the like. It is true that the Communists do not play by our rules. They will not acknowledge our ethical norms as legitimate or binding, and they will not honor the religious and metaphysical convictions behind these ethical norms. They are immune to purely moral suasion; and we do not have it in us to exercise that power in its purity, whatever that might be. But the conflict engages human beings, all of whom fall short of the glory of God. Whatever short-run gains we may hope to reap by interpreting our enemies as mere simulacra of men will do us eventually immeasurable harm. What we thus do to enemies, we often do as well to those whom we would compel or persuade to alliance with us. The "masses" of India or Africa are not so many statistical integers to be written down as assets or liabilities, to be won or lost by our calculation. They are people. Many of them have only the vaguest notions concerning our institutions. Many of them do not care for what they see when they look at us and our institutions. Therefore, we cannot extract pledges from them to throw everything they have into our defense. The full invitation to alliance should read: Let us look beyond the years of warfare, cold and hot, toward the possibilities of new community. To proffer such an invitation in earnest means that we must be prepared to submit our own institutions to whatever far-reaching modification the committed pursuit of that community may demand.

THE WORLD AND THE KINGDOM

The choice here is not between change and no-change. All institutions change; all are fully exposed to the ravages of time, the mighty river. But this is no assurance that the changes are for the better. Only profoundly disciplined intelligence, will, and emotion can assure change that is also real growth. The requisite discipline is the steady and devoted attendance upon the kingdom of God in our midst and over against us. This is the burden of the church's message to the world.

The proclamation of the Kingdom is, then, the very antithesis of any counsel of despair. Though our world is surely cracking at vital points, new possibilities are being thrust upon us from beyond. Terrifying risks accompany these possiblities. Anxious hands may wreak fearful ruination quite as easily as reckless or cruel ones. For this anxiety there is no worldly hope of cure, because it roots in a sickness deeper than the arts of civilization can effectively reach, either for understanding or for cure. The anxiety is ultimately fear for self and world before a God grasped only in pure transcendence. The love of God the Father Almighty can alone liberate us from this mortal terror, this cold sweat of earthly anxiousness. Wherefore, the church preaches Jesus Christ as the founder of the divine community of love, and it preaches this through the power of the Holy Spirit, which in that community worketh faith, hope, and love. And the church declares that he who has faith in the living God is alone prepared for tomorrow; he alone who loves God in Christ is prepared to pour out that love for all his brethren. Without this faith and this love the night and the morrow are indeed grim prospects.

The church preaches not Jesus Christ but another, if it fails to make plain that the Kingdom demands from men a loyalty that transcends all worldly loyalties, and a love that transcends all worldly distinctions and discriminations. This we know. What further do we learn from this about the tension between the church and the world?

A person is always a member of a defining community. He is naturally a member of many less-decisively determining communities as well. But he has both his worldly existence and his eternal existence in a defining community relative to the respective mode of existence. Thus, his historical worldly existence is in the defining community called a living or actual culture and in the society which acknowledges that culture. His eternal existence is in the kingdom of Heaven. The problem of the church is how, within worldly existence, a person can be a member of two defining communities at once, because this is what the gospel seems to demand of us all.

Christianity is an organic religion. This means that it is a total way of life, and affords fresh and revolutionary possibilities for human community. The church should make all of this as plain as possible. It is not primarily interested in presenting yet another loyalty somehow to be absorbed into the complex of cultural loyalties. The church's dominant interests are in a productive synthesis of cultural and human interests, and in the focus, the point of decisive orientation, of that synthesis as a whole. This is the sense in which Christianity is shown forth as a total way of life. But the church preaches the gospel also as providing new and revolutionary possibilities for human community. This is the question of the focus, the point of decisive orientation, of the cultural synthesis as a whole. Let us say that the church ought to be the place above and beyond all others where people are persuaded to ask this capital question: Is this life of mine and this world of ours actually open to creative transformation? When we begin to see some real possibility for answering this question affirmatively, the Kingdom is near unto us, because that can happen only when we realize that there is only one essentially defining community, after all. This or that aspect of character and conduct, the forms in which our interests and energies are expressed, can rightly be said to be determined by the cultural community. Our existence as such is in that divine community of creation and redemption and ultimate consummation, the kingdom of God. If, then, these things are true, evangelical concern is not to bring people into the kingdom of God through the ministrations of the church. Since they are already in the Kingdom, as children are already in the world before they are drawn into school, the great business of the church is to show forth the nature of the realm of which we are all participants, so that the law and the Lord thereof may be rightly obeyed, and so that we may all thereby attain "to mature manhood, to the measure of the stature of the fullness of Christ" (Eph. 4:13).

VII

World Revolution and Individual Transformation

THE CHURCH'S MISSION IS TO PREACH AND TO SHOW FORTH God's saving presence and promise for the world. Salvation is in Jesus Christ; and salvation embraces the world understood both as human civilization and as the created order, the cosmos. Here we are concerned primarily with the world of the human enterprise, but there is something to be gained by seeing how in the Christian perspective the salvation of the human world is one element in, and one aspect of, a redemptive activity of cosmic sweep. And what is to be gained thereby is a corrective for the tendency to abstract God's concern for the human world from his all-embracing concern, and to abstract his concern for us from his love for all men.

Salvation is a term more inclusive and positive than the term "redemption." To be redeemed means to be rescued or delivered from something harmful or destructive. Salvation means to be fulfilled, to enjoy perfect communion with that One with whom alone there is perfect consummation of being. But both salvation and redemption stand for radical, essential, and ultimate change in the creature and in the created order as such. Hence the gospel of salvation cannot be preached as a palliative or as any kind of superficial and symptomatic treatment for the condition of the creature.

WORLD REVOLUTION AND INDIVIDUAL TRANSFORMATION

The church that so preaches has lost its commission. It has turned its charter to the wall.

Because salvation is the work of the incarnate Lord, it includes both the Ultimate and the Now. It is God who saves; and God saves by coming into history and the world. "My Father is working still, and I am working." (John 5:17.) Salvation is going on; it is in process. Therefore, the Christian does not say that he is saved. He says that he is under the promise of salvation. But he is enabled to say also that he is caught up in the initiatory phases of salvation. He lives in the Now of salvation.

To live in the Now of salvation is to live toward the Ultimate, in hope and with great expectations. The church is commissioned to preach both the Now and the Ultimate. But the Ultimate is to be preached as an actuality, not as the ideal fulfillment of an imperfect present situation. The Ultimate is not simply "out there," "ahead of us," in the "great beyond of the future" it is also "up there," above and overspanning us. The Now is sustained by the Ultimate. Specifically, we live not by our hope, psychologically and subjectively regarded, but by a sustaining actuality.

The Now of salvation comprehends both world revolution and personal (individual) transformation. In every period of history God is active, effecting revolution and transformation. The problem is how to distinguish the divine revolution from the human; and the divine transformation of persons from their own efforts to improve and aggrandize themselves.

In this country the proclamation of the gospel as revolutionary is becoming harder by the hour. Naturally we are profoundly suspicious of the communist style of revolution. Many voices are encouraging us to let this suspicion infect our whole understanding of and attitude toward revolution itself. The revolutionary spirit is portrayed as the victim of demonic excitation; or perhaps he is the victim of childhood malnutrition or parental tyranny. Increasingly he is regarded as an alien substance in the clear soup of Americanism and Christianity.

It is true that the revolutionary has made his own contribution to our confusion by deifying his activities and his principles. Watch me, he has seemed to say, and you will see the divine revolution. But the church's God-given message should help our world to discern the error in this, by the positive proclamation of the true revolution.

The divine revolution which is the Now of salvation involves the fundamentally important structures and patterns of our civilization and of all contemporary civilizations. These are the structures which not only exhibit the essence of that civilization, but which also reveal the ontological judgments and intuitions of that civilization. The divine revolution attacks the irrationality, inequity, and rigidity of these structures; and it attacks the provinciality of the ontological judgments and intuitions upon which these structures rest. We cannot say that this revolution has as its aim making these structures and patterns conform to specific ideal patterns in the mind of God. Where this is believed to be the aim, we are only one short step away from fanaticism—from the deadly state of mind which arrogates infallibility to itself. Accordingly, this belief is all of a piece with the vital flaw in man-made revolutions: the proposal to make social structures and personal wills conform to specific ideal patterns in the mind of the revolutionist. What or who will not, or cannot, so conform must be sacrificed; and for these recalcitrants the revolutionist sheds none of the tears that fall so freely for the downtrodden. He loves those whom he can help, and he hates those who threaten to obstruct the program. But he loves above all the ideal patterns and the glowing images. Real people are consistently and perversely less satisfactory—at least until they are made over.

WORLD REVOLUTION AND INDIVIDUAL TRANSFORMATION

The revolutionist habitually wants to substitute one set and kind of social structure for another. He assumes that when this has been accomplished, he will have then but to defend the new system against wicked enemies, within and without, who hate the true good. In this defense he can exhibit a terrible ferocity.

Actually the revolutionist defines his principles and program only in small part by reference to the ideal. For the larger part his position is defined by its polar opposition to the extreme conservatives, that is, to the people who look upon the existent order as divinely ordained in principle and in significant detail and who therefore attack every proposal of change, whether moderate or extreme, as motivated either by ignorance of the true good or by sheer perversity. It requires less than heavenly illumination to see that these people are, in the main, the heavy beneficiaries of the regnant order and the people who believe, without visible grounds, that the heavy beneficiaries deserve all that they derive from the system. The extreme conservatives are also entirely capable of defending the system with remarkable ferocity and with every weapon imaginable, both psychological and physical.

Thus our human revolutions are bred in great violence and are attended regularly by the same. And reason, justice, and freedom, so hotly invoked and adored by all parties to these conflicts, are demigods without residence and without portfolio.

The divine revolution is not like our revolutions; and our revolutions are not necessarily integral and positive elements of the revolution which is the Now of salvation. God's revolution is far more radical than these: it goes to the very foundations of the world. By it we are constrained to see that none of our social structures, actual or ideal, is immune to change, destruction, and revision. In this life we do not build for eternity. None of our work has genuine everlastingness in its own right and through its own power. We are called rather to form social structures that will be relatively responsive to the needs and the possibilities of real persons embraced by the present order. But this really means that we are called to assume and make our own an attitude toward the human world extraordinarily hard both to assume initially and to sustain. This attitude has two elements: All of these structures and patterns are man-made, and all are made for man; and the human world is erected not upon immovable terra firma but upon a river or a sea. The necessities of change and development are not accidentally imposed or encountered: they are in the very nature of things and so are grounded in the will of God.

This dual attitude toward the human world is produced and sustained in us by the divine revolution itself. Certainly we do not habitually so regard civilization, or at any rate our own civilization. It is far easier to look upon the triumphs and the disasters of other civilizations and peoples in history as providential preparation for our own, which, being at last achieved, brings to an end the processes of essential change. What enormous demands are therefore laid upon imagination and upon sanity if we are to see this world of ours, this dearly-beloved common life, as a bridge to the future, as already in process of being overcome and surpassed! When such a thing is proposed to us, we rush to the barricades; we look about to discern an enemy so formidably endowed; and we become feverishly suspicious of any voice crying in the wilderness, "Repent, for the kingdom of heaven is at hand!" Actually, the future does not belong to the enemies of our civilization any more than the present really belongs to us. The Ultimate Enemy is leveling the "artillery of time," not at whatever is good in our world, not at whatever is the honest and humane work of our spirits, but at everything that corrupts and cripples and distorts the spirit of man. If we have built such things into our civilization, as assuredly we have, it will surely suffer grievously ere it dies. Yet the Ultimate Enemy is above all the Healer. What he desires is that we should soberly and reasonably, as well as in fear and trembling, set ourselves to the transformation of our world.

The task of transformation is the task of exploiting to the full the potentialities inherent in the structures and processes of our civilization and society. In this effort these patterns and processes will inevitably be themselves significantly modified. The modification or revolution thus imposed will reflect more of reason than of impulse, more of wisdom than of superstition, more of responsibility than of lust for power.

By way of illustration here, let us consider the aim of Christian participation in politics in this country. The first thing we note is that there is a structure, the existence and nature of which must be acknowledged: the two-party system. We of this generation have inherited this from past generations, and whether we like it or not, there it is, massive and enduring, if not quite incorruptible. Even if we believe that it is ineffective, irrational, and unjust in general or in a particular situation, our protest against it can be effectively registered only by some kind of concrete involvement with it. Efficacious protest requires of us nothing less. If we aspire to political power and influence, we have to work within this system. And we can have no doubt that the key positions are already occupied. The incumbents will not move out simply because we want to move in. We have to bring pressure to bear upon them. As Christians, we feel that there are pressures and weapons we cannot conscientiously use for this purpose. But if we go into the struggle unarmed altogether, and naked except for high resolve, we are asking for what we will surely get—a quick, though not necessarily a painless, political death. But suppose we do somehow get into positions of real power. Now what? Do we have it in mind to use the existing political instrumentalities to attack economic inequities or social ills? Then we must practice the art of the possible and not content ourselves with advocating charming but wholly infeasible programs. But, on the other hand, we cannot assume that these political instrumentalities are either not worthy or not susceptible of modification. They will change. The question is, in what directions and in response to what pressures will they change? The more serious we are in respect to our high calling as politicians, the more determined we will be to participate in these processes determining these changes, and to propose and seek to institute such changes as the moral ends of our efforts suggest and demand.

These proposals must fall within the boundaries of the possible. If anything can be said to be an iron rule of politics, this is it. The "possible" means what can be conceived and effectuated as a natural inheritor of the present system or of some particular important aspect of the present system. Willy-nilly the present system will have an inheritor system. It is not ordained and determined that between the present and the future there shall be stability and rationality of transition. It is only ordained that there will be a transition. And it is also ordained that a person or a race or generation of persons shall not be treated as a mere means for the achievement of another person or generation or race. The actual transitions we are obliged to work out. To work them out calls for the last ounce of devotion and for the highest discipline of the practical reason. Even these may not avail to effectuate orderly and humane transitions; but noble failure is not total loss; and the politician cannot afford to let the possibility of final failure capture his imagination or paralyze his will. The vision of tragedy and death he would do well to leave to the poet, the prophet, or the philosopher. Where the politician finds this impossible, deeply tragic and poignant figures emerge—Abraham Lincoln, Marcus Aurelius.

The divine revolution is God grasping our spirits and disclosing realms of possibility beyond "the boundaries of the possible," in the sense in which this phrase has just been used. In part this means that the possibilities for man are not limited to the possibilities of this present social order or to its natural inheritor or to its competitors and their natural inheritors. These possibilities may not be available now for practical choice of realization. They may be available only for the kind of envisagement that edifies, that uplifts the spirit and enkindles the poetic imagination. Thus men have dreamed of a land fairer than any that ever was; and of a race loftier than any that has ever been. Under the spell of these dreams men may act as though they were native citizens of that land and only strangers here, descended from that marvelous breed, and only distant cousins, if kin at all, of all worldlings.

But the possibilities urged upon us by the divine revolution are not exhausted by the poet. The prophet is caught up in that revolution—indeed, without that revolution the prophet is unthinkable, just as under the power of that revolution he is unbearable. It is the prophet who expresses most vividly the involvement of civilization with a community both all-comprehensive and purely (that is, in its own right and through itself) everlasting. It is the prophet who teaches most authoritatively of all human teachers that, though all creatures and all creaturely things are mortal, it is given to us human creatures *to die forward* with our creations. Die we must, and our world lies under the same sentence; but we may die toward—what? Not toward a moral order that is merely the balloon of our aspirations inflated and cut free of every time and place. We may die toward One who holds together this Now, out of which we perish, and the Ultimate, in which his whole creation rejoices together!

It is from this vision of the living God that the prophet derives whatever he has to say about the awful defection of civilization from truth, righteousness, and creativity. His standard of moral judgment is not ideal; it is God himself, supremely and transcendently actual both in and beyond this Now.

Where does the church stand in relation to the divine revolution and to the transformation of our civilization? What a hard vocation it has—a vocation hard and hazardous because it combines roles that in any normal calculation appear to be mutually irreconcilable: the political and the prophetic. To say that the church has a political role is not to say that the church is itself an administrator of the civil order. The responsibility of the church is so to preach the gospel that men will see their responsibilities in that order and themselves seek to soften its inflexibilities, in order that its decrees and its structures should be rational rather than arbitrary, humane rather than mechanical. And what is the prophetic role of the church? Hardly to distract and bemuse the present age with passionate but irrelevant condemnations, or to arouse the age to the pursuit of possibilities properly susceptible of poetic envisagement alone. Prophecy concerns the Now of the divine revolution. It reminds us that there is no permanent solution to our problems, no solution prescriptible in formula and dogma. These formulas have varying degrees of relevancy, and we can determine the particular degree only by patient investigation. Finally, in its prophetic role the church declares that even as we work away at the problems inherent in our civilization we must have and we do have solid footing on which to stand

WORLD REVOLUTION AND INDIVIDUAL TRANSFORMATION

as we do this work. This solid footing is no institution, and it is no institutional fiat. The solid ground is the divine community, of which we are members, not by inheritance or by merit, but by creation and by grace.

Now it is time to remember that we American Protestant Christians have a very deeply engrained habit of thought. We believe that the divine revolution concerns persons considered as individuals having their existences and their characters apart from their relationships to one another and to history. We usually say that only if these individuals are transformed is there any hope for the transformation of society. And we conclude, therefore, that the church must try above all else to change hearts. Changed hearts can transform civilization.

This should be called the sniper approach to the church's mission. The sniper is detailed to pick off the enemy one by one. If he is uncommonly lucky, he may bag an officer of some importance; but even so he adds up his score one man at a time until he in turn becomes a score in another sniper's record. But, of course, major elements of a campaign or of a battle are not committed to the snipers. They have nuisance value, but the strategic plan is far more comprehensive than anything conceivably open to successful actualization by sniper activity alone.

The Protestant church in the modern world apparently does not know this limitation inherent in sniper action, for here the rule seems to be: pick them off one by one, and if you can pile up a very heavy score, you can change the world! Strategic plans ostensibly more comprehensive are in fact tactical maneuvers calculated to bring more targets under the fire of the snipers. Local action of this sort sometimes creates the passing impression of being a major engagement, but at best it is a diversionary or screening action. The decisive engagement is occurring elsewhere.

Aha, we say, but the gospel demand for repentance is clearly addressed to individual persons, is it not? Yes, that is certainly the case. But the persons so addressed are real persons whose hearts are deeply and inalienably involved with the world. That change of heart which is the divine revolution within the citadel of personal freedom and responsibility, did and does change the world: the pattern of relations embracing the heart and its world is itself converted or transformed. "Perfect love casts out fear"; "We walk not according to the flesh but according to the Spirit" —these are ways of saying that the power of God in Jesus Christ makes the heart fit and ready to cope productively with the world, which to do is its calling and its duty.

Hence we conclude that the transformation of the individual person *is* part of the plan of salvation. The power for his regeneration is released within and upon him, in order to draw him into this plan as an integral and productive participant. This is the Now of God's saving revolution. The outward mark of the saving Presence is the expansion of moral horizons; the inner mark, a growing satisfaction in seeking that inclusive community and in finding within it profound affinities with persons as persons.

Growth, change, regeneration, promise, hope: these are the "manifest" of salvation. Men are not drawn in this life into the Ultimate of salvation. Of the Ultimate there is but a foretaste, but it is enough and more than enough to leaven the lump of selfishness, perversity, and darkness in us all. The church is not to be thought of, therefore, as the place where people are miraculously shorn of their sins. It is the place where, by the miracle of Christ's love, people learn to take deepening responsibility for other sinners. It is not in the church of Christ that we are enjoined to count on the occurrence of the impossible for ourselves; but it is there we learn what is possible in the Now of salvation and what is

WORLD REVOLUTION AND INDIVIDUAL TRANSFORMATION

the Ultimate toward which the whole creation presses with infinite longing.

The transformation of our world and the regeneration of ourselves—these are a unity in the Now which the church is chartered to proclaim when it says: Now is "the acceptable year of the Lord!"

VIII

Evangelical Zeal and Cultural Pride

ZEAL FOR THE KINGDOM IS THE DEFINING PASSION OF THE Christian church so far as it is faithful to its charter. To be about the Father's business and to be about it with holy and triumphant passion: this is the church's calling.

This passion is prompted and sustained alone by God's revelation and our acknowledgment of the Word of redemption and salvation. When the church no longer professes to know what the Father's business is, or when it professes to believe that something else is more important, zeal for the Kingdom fades away. But of course the church nowhere makes overt and witting confession that it has fallen into either of these conditions. Piety and self-righteousness—surely a formidable marriage—prohibit such a confession. Actually, either of these conditions may prevail. Against this there is no supernatural guarantee.

Zeal for the gospel and the Kingdom is compounded of three elements. The first of these is love of persons as persons, as the sons and daughters of God. This is very different from love in which we respond only or primarily to our own image projected upon those whom we profess to love. To love one's own image is either to love oneself in or through the other, or it is to see the other through the image of a person whom one regards, perhaps quite unconsciously, as irresistibly demanding or soliciting love. The latter is also

EVANGELICAL ZEAL AND CULTURAL PRIDE

a form of self-love, because here also the hope is that the other so loved will repay this love in one way or another. Furthermore, the love which figures in the zeal for the Kingdom is also very different from the love which accepts or even embraces unnatural limitations upon its exercise and its quality. Since God acts in Jesus Christ for the salvation of all his children, we must believe that he loves them all equally. This is something far easier to profess with the lips than to believe in the heart and to assimilate into the springs of action. But it is Christ's demand that we express so great and inclusive a love. Who does not do so, or who does not aspire to do so, does not love God.

This love which God has spread abroad in our hearts has a deep and lasting quarrel with methods of doing the church's business which compromise, when they do not violate, the essential integrity and freedom of persons. Evangelistic programs which slavishly incorporate techniques and attitudes of supersalesmanship are a good case in point. Resort to these illicit weapons is often dictated by concentration on quick and visible returns, and is often justified by claiming that people have got to be "sold" a gospel which they really need, whether or not they are really aware of the need.

The second element compounded in true evangelical zeal is obedience to God. God commands the church to proclaim the good news of the Kingdom; and what God commands who will refuse? "You did not choose me, but I chose you" holds as fully and firmly for God's covenant with the church as it held for his covenant with Israel. The church does not establish itself; it is established by the Word spoken to it and through it. This Word is spoken to it from on high; it is something that comes to the church from beyond the church and from beyond history and from beyond the world. And though the Word is truly given into the world and into history, it is still God's Word;

it is still and everlastingly God. Therefore, the church has no effective choice before the Word except to be humble and obedient. The church does indeed make, or seek to make, other choices, but in respect to its calling and its commission these other choices are demonstrably nonefficacious. Presently we shall be occupied with this demonstration.

Evangelical zeal is compounded of a third element: conviction that the *Now of salvation is upon us*. This conviction grows out of a real laying hold of the Word in which the living God reveals himself and his redemptive purpose and power. "The field is white for the harvest; the winnowing fan is in the Harvester's hand!" All men and the whole world are the whited fields of the Harvester. Let us therefore make haste to publish the glad tidings far and wide. Let us bid all men to prepare themselves and to be unremittingly vigilant and alert.

Here we have to reckon with something more demanding and incomparably more promising than the causes which we promote with fractional loyalty and transitory enthusiasm. The Kingdom is not just another interesting church-promotion program to be realized if and when the official board decides to do so. There is no *might be* for the Kingdom. *It is* and *it will be*. Neither is there anything problematical or precarious about its value. It is that pearl of great price for the possession of which any resolute and knowledgeable man will gladly give all that he can call his own.

It would appear entirely just to suppose, then, that the church would enter into its vocation and into the performance of its mighty tasks with an inspired self-forgetfulness, sacrificing joyously all worldly concerns and aspirations. What word should we expect to hear more frequently and more sincerely and faithfully uttered by the church than, "For me to die is gain!" And in fact there are those sublime moments in its history when this expectation is wonderfully fulfilled. By the grace of God there are such moments. But moments they are. They do not define that history, however greatly they elevate and dignify it. In the main that history is much different. Its story is one of involvement and complicity with the world which the church is supposed to be in but not of—involvement so profound and so systematic that the sole visible element of transcendence of the world has been a capacity for idealizing possibilities suggested by the world but not at a given moment actually realized.

Distinguished from pious expectations and from every delusion born of outraged conscience, the actual situation of the church is one of inextricable involvement with the world. The church is one institution among many in our society. It is caught fast in a highly competitive situation, even though its competitors are not always clearly identified as such. In all its life the church is fully exposed to the workings of cultural pride.

Cultural pride has two principal forms in the church: A pride in its own internal life and value; a pride in the environing and inclusive culture. These expressions of cultural pride are generally intermixed in any concrete situation. Yet we may gain something by inspecting each as though it were a separate phenomenon.

1. The church has a manifest pride in its own intramural culture. To the world it says: Here is a distinctive way of life with unique satisfactions and unique order. And it says also to the world: This life in the church is a better one than anything attainable in the outside world. But at once we sense very serious oversights, as well as other weaknesses, in these claims. For instance, how can the life in the church be interpreted as an inclusive enterprise, that is, as being a culture on its own and by itself? It is a plain matter of fact that our whole existence is not in the church. Our daily work is not in it; our daily work is not for the church in any obvious way. Relatively little time is devoted to the

church, except of course for the professionals who are paid, after a fashion, to keep it going. If the church affects people at large at all, it does so on the periphery of existence and aspiration.

Actually this first form of cultural pride is very seldom encountered in the naked way in which it is expressed above. The attitude is much more commonly expressed in these ways: (a) There are in the church's life certain specific activities, attitudes, and principles which are more significant than anything in the outside world. For instance, the church's worship, its moral attitudes, and ethical principles. (b) So far as the outside world is good at all, it is a reflection of the church's life. Hence, the world must look to the church for moral and spiritual guidance.

This latter conviction is well on its way toward identification with the second main form of cultural pride. It does not always get there. Many things can prevent its safe arrival, such as the counterconviction that the world—civilization in general—can never adequately express or embody what is present in purity in the church. Perhaps this is simply because the world is too large and complex, whereas moral and spiritual purity requires a small, homogeneous, face-to-face community. But perhaps, on the other hand, in the world wicked and ungodly men inevitably hold the whip hand and hog the driver's seat. The world is the devil's home park in which he never loses.

In these ways the people of the church may express and reinforce their pride in the elevation and distinctiveness of life within the church.

2. The second main form of the church's cultural pride shows this pride reaching out to embrace lovingly Christian civilization and culture. To call a culture and a society "Christian" is in itself an expression of this pride.

There are many expressions of this state of mind in our present situation in the church. The church takes credit for being the source and inspiration of Western culture. Whatsoever things are pure, whatsoever things are good—these are the dowry invested in our world by the church.

Today the church also assumes the role of guardian of our civilization. Wicked enemies are abroad, and they must be rightly identified and sturdily resisted. Such weapons as the church herself uses in this great conflict must be consonant with her spiritual character, to be sure. Wide latitude prevails within this restriction, as well as wide latitude in the interpretation of the restriction itself.

The church evinces pride in the world by voluntarily and eagerly assuming a priestly role in and for our civilization. The priestly office is administered in behalf both of the victims and of the victimizers within our society. The victims are thereby assured that somebody loves them, after all. They are also pointedly enjoined to be reconciled to the realities of the order rather than to waste themselves in futile revolt against it.

The priestly office has ritual at its command. This ritual is the formalized gestures of philanthropic and paternalistic solicitude. These are ritualistic gestures because they are presumed to have an efficacy vastly larger than their immediate effects and because this efficacy is presumably released by the gesture itself. Everyone who makes one of these gestures knows very well that it is but a pin-point drop of oil on a vast and troubled sea. Yet the pin-point drop is supposed to have efficacy stretching beyond the horizon. The recreation room provided and furnished for neighborhood juvenile delinquents is supposed to reconstitute their existence from the ground up, and point a shining way to their whole kind. The friendly smile for the Negro porter is supposed to explode the fearful log jams of exploitation and resentment, and let the spirit of brotherhood come sluicing down in healing streams, carefully channeled and regulated.

As for the victimizers, the church is their priest, whether or not they know it and are properly grateful. They are absolved of their sins in several directions at once. There is the direction of exculpation: the victimizers are simply administrators of a system which they did not create and which they cannot change. And there is also the direction of reasonable penance: they may be reasonably required to make public confession that spiritual values are more significant than worldly goods, and they may be reasonably expected to use part of their worldly goods to feed the poor. If the latter penance is performed through the good offices of the church, the statistical effect is gratifying.

The church is the priest of Christian civilization because it is more largely responsible than any other institution for the elaboration and defense of these cultural rituals.

But now the vision of yet another role arises in a few troubled and anxious minds. Perhaps the church is destined again to be the last asylum of our civilization. Suppose that our civilization should be inundated by barbarians. Would the church become an archive for humane ideals and for oddments of scientific law and of art, until barbarism fell to pieces and a new order should appear in the ruins of the old? There are few of us Americans who traffic in such visions, though elsewhere these visions receive a more sympathetic welcome. We are confident of tomorrow. There may be great problems, but initiative and resolution will master them. And so here the church has a positive work to do, the work of providing goals for our vitality, and easement for our occasional flashes of bad conscience.

In all of these ways the church evinces a great pride in this civilization. The church is in the world and, most emphatically, it is of the substance of the world. What then becomes of the zeal for the gospel and the Kingdom? How then shall that God be worshiped and served before whom

EVANGELICAL ZEAL AND CULTURAL PRIDE

all are sinners and before whom our national self-love is blasphemy?

Well, we can see plainly that the church is very zealous to build itself up. There is great zeal in this department. Evangelistic enterprises are programs of zealous ecclesiastical aggrandizement. On occasion they may be more than that, but when are they ever less? Certainly not when the program is "interdenominational." What carries a particular church into such an effort if it is not the hope that it will thereby reap a bountiful harvest for itself? To be sure, the watchword is, Save Souls! A soul thus rescued counts for nought unless translated into a statistic in some report.

In this zeal for its own aggrandizement the church advertises its contributions to culture. It elicits support and loyalty for itself on the ground that it is a repository and guardian of moral and spiritual values. This seems to be a unique claim, one that competitor institutions cannot make with comparable validity or with so straight a face. People are asked by the church: "Do you want to know what makes for a meaningful and truly successful life? If you do, join the church, support the church." What other institution in our society makes such claims for itself?

Zeal in pursuing its own ends leads the church naturally to imitate the methods of institutions competing with it in our society. The church turns its evangelists into salesmen, equipped with the latest stereotypes pertaining to the effective promoting and merchandising of a product. The pastoral or layman's call should be brisk, vivid, businesslike, and decision compelling. The sound evangelist will learn to read the signs of sales resistance, and either take another tack or close out the conversation before the person can make articulate and decisive his objections or his questions. What the church has to "sell" must be something that can be put in a cheerful and attractive package. Its product must be obviously usable to the point of indispensability and far beyond. The minister also must show that he is a good manager, a real executive. The shepherd is really an administrator thoroughly familiar with the principles of efficient organization.

We are moved now to ask whether in all of this the church has not made a choice to be something other than a humble and obedient servant of Christ, that Word of God from beyond which is yet in our midst. If this means a clear and self-conscious choice, the answer is No. If it means a really effective choice, the answer is again No. The church has always had to fight the battle of cultural pride, in one form or another; and the battle has always been an ambiguous one. Called into the world to proclaim the gospel of salvation, the people of the church have always lived deeply involved with the world from which they are called out. Sometimes they are proud of that involvement. Sometimes they are ashamed of it. In either case they participate in the substance of that world to which salvation is published. Their essential situation is not different from that of other men. Even when salvation is grasped as aimed directly and personally at them, they are indecisive and irresolute creatures. They have courage and insight spasmodically. Their aspirations are commonly built upon illusions; and they apprehend the realities with horror. These are the people of the church. So to be is to be human. And thus again we say: the gospel is not ours; it is God's. We can take no credit for it. The glory shining in it is no glory of ours: it is the glory of the only Son of God the Almighty Father. We may work to draw out of the gospel a social philosophy, a complete ethic; and we may design to sell these by-products complete with adulterations built in, as the whole gospel or as the simple gospel. To be sure, as Christian we must formulate such a philosophy and ethic; but the gospel is incomparably greater than all these necessary by-products, and in the end they fall away before it. This is what is happening all around us today, if we would but see it. The church is finding it necessary to learn humility and obedience before the living Word, all over again.

It is the hard way to learn, yes. But is there any other? The church made a confused choice to serve its own ends. This choice was not a very effective one, for by it the church accepted for the gospel an incidental role and place in the world, and it has come finally to occupy just such an incidental place itself. To be the humble and obedient servant of Jesus Christ is a very different matter. Then the church is no longer much concerned with its status in the world. It is no longer bothered by the question whether people are saying nice things about it. One all-consuming passion fills its frame—to be spent for the glory of the Kingdom.

Now and again this spirit overcomes the church—and what a beautiful and powerful and truth-loving creature it is then! Perhaps this will happen to the church in our world, and to us in the church. Perhaps it is already happening as we feel ourselves drawn into the race with time. For this is a race which strips away the nonessentials. Moreover, we cannot run it looking backward to the glories of a Christian civilization; and we cannot run it looking sideways at illusory castles floating in rosy cloudlands; and we cannot run it looking downward at the pitfalls and abysses beneath our feet. This race with time we can run only by looking to the living Word, Jesus Christ, the author and the perfecter of our faith.

IX

The Race with Time

THE DISTINCTION BETWEEN EVANGELICAL ZEAL AND CULtural pride seems proper and necessary in peaceful and settled times. In a profoundly troubled time such a distinction may appear both abstract and dangerous. It may seem dangerous so far as it threatens to diminish the enthusiasm with which we defend our society and its culture. The men of a fire company do not pause, when called out, to inquire among themselves whether the object of their concern is really worth all this trouble. When we are summoned to the defense of our society, can we afford to inquire whether we thus fulfill the perfect will of God? At just such a time the demands of the gospel and the exigencies of our situation in the world seem to coincide most completely. We have the sense of having come upon one of the great turning points in world history. We breathe the air of cultural crisis. And thus the mood is ripe for the planting of that word: the end is at hand, *unless*. Unless what? Unless we commit everything to the struggle with a powerful and insidiously cunning enemy.

It is not an accident that the eschatology of the gospel should have been rediscovered in a great crisis of Western life. Each successive generation sees itself and its great problems reflected in the gospel. We are no exception. We are greatly puzzled as to how our fathers could have been so insensitive to the End, which we apprehend everywhere in the gospel, and everywhere as formidable. But our fathers

THE RACE WITH TIME

were not involved in the race with time, not as we are. For them time was a friend. They named it creative evolution, productive process—and these were all love names. Time was a mother-wife, inexhaustibly fecund. Time was a mistress who would never grow old and jaded. Every high resolve and every productive purpose would find its time. The time horizon both for mankind and for the individual person was both far away and friendly. For mankind there was the hope of progress without arbitrary terminus in history. For the individual person there was the immortal soul triumphant over the termination of mere bodily activity.

Time, for our fathers' children, has again become the "ever-rolling stream that bears its sons away," including its lovers and its worshipers. There is not time enough for all that we would do and become. The time horizon is closing in, and it seems not so amiable. The individual person has to reckon with his own death as being more than the mere termination of bodily activity. Indeed, we are preoccupied with death, and little wonder, since twice in one generation our world has been converted into a charnel house. And so far as mankind is concerned, science appears to teach us that there is a total terminus in sight, even if man resists the temptation to destroy himself. To be sure, science is dealing here with a rather impressive spread of time, so far as any one person is concerned; but the spread of time is presumed to include the flickering out of the whole human enterprise on earth. Thus Everyman can tell himself as he reflects upon his own death, that Lastman—however far out in time he may be—will be in no better case.

This wider cosmological dimension is admittedly abstract, so far as the concrete human situation is concerned. It does not chill us so effectively as the hazards of the short run. Everyman is now encouraged to think of himself as Lastman, *unless!*

TOWARD A THEOLOGY OF EVANGELISM

This monumental *unless* marks the great divide separating the time of the world from the time of the gospel. In the gospel the proclamation is unqualified: the End is at hand. Preoccupied with the fate of the dearly beloved world and the dearly beloved self, we always add: *unless*. Thereby we turn away from the demands of the gospel and from the instancy of the Kingdom, back toward a total involvement with the exigencies of worldly existence. It is at this point that the church of Jesus Christ faces a most difficult task. It must preach the instancy of the Kingdom. To do so is God's demand. But the church must also preach, as an integral part of this message, that obedience to the Kingdom promises redemption from morbid preoccupation with the time of the world. Our present task is to elaborate the meaning of this redemption.

The time of the world must be distinguished from *astronomical* time and from *psychological* time. Psychological time is directly perceived, or felt, duration. Duration is broken up into "equal" parts for certain limited purposes; and these equal parts are registered on clocks and calendars. Clocks and calendars are transparent frauds, but they are useful ones. Astronomical time, on the other hand, has very little to do with felt duration. It is more nearly a conceptual relationship, something by definition incapable of direct perception, even though imaginative representations of it are sometimes made, for example, how many lifetimes you would have to live through to reach a certain star. The only really significant contact with felt duration made by astronomical time appears to be in the definition of the velocity of light. But even here the contact is not with duration but with clock time.

The time of the world is the pressure exerted upon duration or felt time by the society and the culture in which a person lives. The targets of this pressure are the will primarily and the intellect secondarily. Let us see how this works out.

Will is our choice-making power. Intellect is our power of knowing. Every society tries to instruct and to mold these powers in such a way that the person's decisions will sustain and enhance that society. Thus there is a time in which to do certain things and in which not to do or even to want certain others. These times can become occasions of great tension in the person. His powers of feeling may not be up to these social demands. The time externally and arbitrarily defined as appropriate may fail abysmally to register in the person. If he is reduced to mechanical acquiescence to these external demands, he is worthless as a creative agent. If he refuses altogether to assimilate these demands into himself as a responsible person, he is potentially a destroyer of society. An equilibrium of forces is therefore required. This is brought about by making the external demands appear to be internal promptings: the worker looks at the clock and decides that he is hungry; the lover looks at the clock and sees that he ought to be going home.

Clock and calendar are social instruments for the measurement of acceptable and productive activity. By them the person can determine when he will be given time-off for good behavior, that is, when he will be given time to enjoy without measurement. In our society and culture this time-off is largely illusory. The preachment that what a man does with his spare time is his own business is at least misleading and perhaps simply false. The pressures remain during his time-off. He is reminded that his entertainment should be legitimate and upbuilding. His recreation should still leave him open to solicitation to consume the goods and services which keep the wheels of the economy turning. He should do something productive with his leisure time; it should be organized, directed, and evaluated. Over all of life in our culture the shadows of the clock and the calendar fall.

The technological revolution, hardly more than fairly begun, even now presents the industrial worker, and eventually it will present all of us, with great swatches of "free time." This is a reward for having become the servant of the machine. But society is afraid of what it has done. The individual is not to be left to himself and to his own resources. And so time, his own time, his free time, is corrupted into anxiety; and his personal resources are bankrupted; and he flees for assurance and solace to the crowd. He wants above all else to be accepted by that redeeming crowd. To achieve this he must repudiate the slightest interest in nonconformity. He is schooled to examine every preachment, whether from pulpit or editorial page, for its orthodoxy. The final iron-headed and peace-splintering shaft, driven and pounded into his spirit, is this: this is a free country, here you can think and talk as you please! But to think (an activity not to be confused with the process of keeping prejudices in constant circulation through one's mind) requires untrammeled solitude.[1] Is our society willing to grant this fundamental prerequisite for thinking? Again, to think as one pleases requires a twofold freedom of enquiry: (1) There must be free access to alternative viewpoints on decisive questions. It is not enough to be told that certain of these are so wrong he need not bother with them. (2) There must be freedom of expression, because

---

[1] This solitude is not necessarily physical isolation. It is the opportunity to examine patiently and dispassionately whatever rises to the surface of the mind. Solitude is the time of personal reflection. As such it should be carefully distinguished from loneliness, which is a feeling state, or feeling quality. Perhaps this confusion has something to do with the widespread reluctance to embrace solitude. But perhaps there is also the fear that the time of personal reflection will find one with nothing to reflect upon, except the hunger to be lost in the crowd.

only when viewpoints are expressed do their errors and defects come to light.

It is hard in this present not to feel that the lid is being screwed down upon these freedoms. The boundaries of appropriate expression of thought narrow alarmingly. And as they do so, the juice of real freedom to exist as a unique person will be squeezed out. That existence will seem to be pre-eminently desirable in which we all become persons anonymous.

In this situation and with all that it portends, the churches are commonly instruments in the hands of culture. The churches declare that the crisis is essentially a moral and spiritual one. This generally means: Our institutions are founded upon and are direct expressions of certain cosmic moral laws; we have lately been negligent in respect to obedience to these laws and therefore our institutions are in grave peril; this peril can be reduced, if not eliminated altogether, by fresh access of piety before the moral law. One thinks particularly here of the presidential campaign of 1952, with its vague appeals to moral and spiritual values.

No other preachment could so clearly point to the certificate given to the church by our society—a certificate for meritorious service. But what happens to the people who receive this vague moralistic proclamation week after week, year after year? What encouragement do they derive from it to face the realities? What demand is registered through it to acknowledge the reality of God's judgment upon all of us and upon all of our ways? What inducement does it provide to seek the Lord whose habitation is not the temple but the broken and the contrite heart? What disclosure is made through it of an end that is radically different from the crack-up of our civilization?

A certificate for meritorious service in behalf of civilization is not to be mistaken for the church's charter. By the terms of that charter the church's message is: This is the acceptable year of the Lord; repent, for the kingdom of God is at hand!

If the church is to proclaim this message it must also, and as a part of the proclamation, set forth what it apprehends as the distinction between worldly time and the time of the Kingdom. What does this involve?

The time of the Kingdom must first be related as directly as possible to personal and concrete time. We have called this time *duration*, which is a directly felt flow. Duration is not perceived as an object. It is grasped as an aspect of activity. Thus time is concretely apprehended as the going on referred to in the statement, "Something is *going on*." For certain purposes we can disengage this "going-on-ness" from the things that are going on, and consider going-on-ness as a kind of container in which the things exist. But this is a feat of abstraction; and we have no good reason to believe that the abstraction is matched by a reality somehow like it. On the other hand, we are certainly not prepared to identify time with simple activity itself (felt activity, that is, activity about which we can say seriously, This is *my activity*). So far as going on has *phases* we say that it *is* (and not simply that it is *in*) time. Each phase flows out of another phase and flows into another phase. For special purposes we can make artificially clear and distinct breaks between these phases. For instance, I could say with some hope of being understood: "I left boyhood behind the day my dog died." And we do very commonly speak in terms such as, "This is the end of this chapter in my life," "This is the end of Roman civilization," and so on. But clarity in such expressions is made possible by artificiality. As actually endured or lived through, there was no such sharply defined culmination of one phase of existence and inauguration of a subsequent phase.

The time of the Kingdom in the gospel makes head-on contact with this concrete time of our real existence. The

THE RACE WITH TIME

Kingdom does not come at us round-about through worldly time but straight down from above. To exist as a real person, as a being whose whole life is bound up in going on, is to be in a realm not ordered and sustained by one's own self nor by all mortal beings taken together. This realm is a reality; its name is eternity.

So far there is no reason for saying that eternity is timeless. It is a realm which embraces time. It is an act, an activity, by which time is constituted and by which it is consummated. Hence, eternity is not a static container for temporal creatures, a cosmic gymnasium in which an incredible indefinitude of goings on leap about. Eternity is being which by its own activity sustains all enduring subjects.

When the church preaches the nearness of the End, it is not talking merely about the future. It is saying something about an Actuality which embraces future and present and past. This Actuality is not getting closer to us in either a temporal or a spatiotemporal sense. By this Actuality our life and our world are being drawn out ever nearer their culmination and their ultimate transfiguration.

A second thing must now be said about this time of the Kingdom. In respect to our time as persons, the time of the Kingdom is summons rather than cause, in any ordinary sense of the term cause. Jesus Christ speaks for freedom and he speaks to freedom. He stands at the door and knocks. He invites us to participate in the blessed life of the Kingdom. And so the church is licensed to extend an invitation, speaking always person-to-person in the name of Jesus Christ. The church is not ordained to assault personal integrity and to compromise personal freedom.

The time of the Kingdom is an invitation, yes; but it is an imperative invitation. It is a summons. The Kingdom comes, whether or not we accept it. We are summoned to decide one way or the other. Decide we must; but the decision arises out of freedom, or it is not a decision for the kingdom of God.

The imperative summons of the Kingdom ought not to be seen as the work of an impatient, time-watching God. Our sin against God is grievous offense, but we have not the slightest warrant for supposing that it prompts an ungodly reaction in God! And if we profess sincerely that we try the divine patience, we also remember that God does not think as we think. Will God's patience run out and will he then call for a bulldozer; or will he make a fatal mark upon the lintel, to instruct his angels: "Waste no time here"? Compared with the poor thing so named in us, God's patience is inexhaustible, for it expresses his sustaining and redeeming love. Though I spurn and flee him, he will have me in the end. Yet in the end he will not simply do something *to* me; he will do something in and through me.

If these things are worthy of acceptation, it follows that the nearness of the Kingdom is not to be so preached that it becomes one more anxiety to be added to the ever-growing heap of anxieties. The appointment with eternity is not to be interpreted as though it were like all the other appointments in this weird and reeling world. The preacher of the gospel of Jesus Christ is not one more insurance salesman come to remind us with professional gravity and not entirely disinterestedly that someday—probably sooner than we think—we too shall die, and therefore that we must act now. Well, how does one act now in relation to death? The ready-made answers, whether of insurance specialist or evangelist too much his counterpart, have all a fatal flaw: we cannot act, really and productively, in relation to an abstract death. We act in relation to (toward) being, not toward not-being. Life is always defined by its ongoing relation to God, to whom we live and to whom we die. Here we must remember divine counsel: Take no thought for tomorrow.

THE RACE WITH TIME

The "tomorrow" for which I might think to take effective provision is, today, a mere thing of the imagination. I can take effective thought of what is going on, and I can anticipate its continuation, its termination, its fulfillment. But the world is not bound by my anticipations. Too much of our time and too much of our substance are expended in the hope of outguessing the world and God. Endlessly we ponder the question, "What will tomorrow bring?" How often this question reveals the emptiness of today; or a today honeycombed with anxiety and terror! We would be better employed with questions more nearly within our grasp. Specifically, the gospel enjoins us to ask and to reflect upon two momentous questions: How clearly in what is now going on in my existence can I grasp the end (the aim and purpose) of my being? Toward what consummation of my existence as a whole am I pointed?

There are occasions when these are infinitely disturbing questions. The present is such an occasion. These questions open to our existence vast uncertainties and deep misgivings, and this at just the time when we need to feel most sure of ourselves and most confident that the moral forces of the universe fight for us. And in the areas of large importance in our culture these questions precipitate us toward the depths of insecurity. I mean the areas of work, of play, and of love.

Let a person ask of his work whether, and how clearly, he can grasp in it the end of his being as a person. What does his work have to do with his being human and with his being *this person?* We can all see that work has something to do with being able to eat and with having a roof (mortgaged) over our heads. These are real goods; but they are not the be-all of a person. And if this is all that his work provides, then his work may well seem to him to be trivial; and his whole life is trivialized if he is convinced that his work is all-important. But suppose that his work is not only trivial but also that in it he is infinitely substitutable—that a nameless and countless horde, each of whom is capable of doing his work, looms always over his shoulder. Shall we wonder when he cracks up and gives way to one of that horde, who in turn will be hounded and harassed into disintegration?

And now let us ask our second question of work: what can a person learn about the consummation of his existence from the work he does? If the immediate consummation of work-purpose is eating, what is the purpose in eating? Obviously, to stay alive. But this obvious answer is quite inadequate in our society. Part of the purpose in eating is to consume the goods we are trying to produce in mounting abundance. Thus a person is an individual consumption machine. And thus a person finds that his fundamental questions concerning his work seem to prompt circular answers. If he tries to break out of this circle, he will stand exposed as a nonconformist. He will be a straight thinker rather than a circle thinker. And such men are dangerous.

Let us turn our questions on the area of play. Play is activity freed from socially productive responsibilities. In play the spirit of man blows any which way—the blowing itself is the thing to be prized. Play may be very strenuous, but the striving is not foreordained to a particular end. Play robbed of this spontaneity and randomness is a mockery, a trivializing and deadly mockery. A society which systematically so defrauds the play of its people is committing itself and them to spiritual sterility.

Has our society so committed itself? There are some clear warnings of this. Even at play we find it hard to forget that we are consumers. The player to be admired is the player properly equipped and accoutered—the good little consumer. Furthermore, the good player is the one who strives for the highest degree of expertness—the image of the omnipresent specialist is projected into play. Do you enjoy bridge? Then you should be constantly improving your game. Why? Do the experts get that much more fun out of their game than we dubs and duffers do out of ours? The question appears to miss the point, which is that the game has certain potentialities that ought to be realized. The game ought to be played right. Thus play becomes encrusted with procedural conventions and with injunctions to conscientious performance. Such a game has become a gleaming little model of the "serious world." When this happens to play, its recreative value hurries off to its vanishing point. When that serious world is supposed itself to be modeled upon eternity, the possibilities of a stultifying and paralyzing anxiety are magnificently proliferated, and play is no release or relief at all.

What do we find when we bring our questions to the realm of love? What can a person in our society hope to grasp that pertains to the end of his existence, from his love life? One thing is obvious at once: love and love-making are not the same. Every schoolboy knows this, it seems, though it is not a matter of formal instruction. To love another person is a demanding activity. It demands an awareness, acute and therefore painful, of actualities. To love demands great effort: to love a person one must struggle to become a person himself. To love means to set out from familiar country into the unknown. But love-making is a very different matter. Love-making is quite compatible with unsullied illusions and phantasies. Indeed where love-making is exalted into an end in itself, illusions and phantasies are its food and drink. Actualities are then carefully side stepped. Responsibility to the other person is then exhausted by a simulated tenderness for the partner's comfort while in the act of love, and in provision for the partner's "satisfaction." The good lover is the man or woman well versed in sexual tactic and technique. The revelations of the love-maker have to do with rare titillations, rare pleasures. To reveal the depth of personal existence would break the amorous spell.

TOWARD A THEOLOGY OF EVANGELISM

There are many inducements in our society to lose ourselves in love-making rather than in love. Love-making is properly open to consumer cultivation: the good love-maker must be appropriately outfitted right down to the skin, and into it. The look, the smell, the touch, must all be standardized. And the standards are all subject to translation into merchandise.

In these ways love-making is also modeled after the serious world. An outrageously adequate love-maker is no real threat to that serious world. If such a person appears on the scene to threaten a particular marriage, the husband or wife, as the case may be, takes a few glamour lessons, or changes his shaving cream, and the threat evaporates. Hence from love-making a person learns that here too he is defined by consumer-producer relations. Activities in this realm do not seem to be calculated to reveal the end of his existence. If by this he would be instructed as to the consummation of his life, what would he learn? Who would be his saints and his paragons?

It is only through love that a person can begin to make out the end of his existence, and it is only by love that he can have an intimation of consummation. This is the actuality. But it is actuality from whose face many turn away in fear, because truly to love is to step out into relationships and activities which culture cannot absolutely determine and in which therefore security is left far behind and below. Bad love can be distinguished from good, to be sure; but who can predict what the issue will be when he begins to love?

Love cannot be successfully modeled after the serious world. The serious world is commonly an escape from love. The give-and-take of love is very different from the world in which self-aggrandizement is held to be the natural law. Little wonder it is, then, that so many profess that they have not the time for love. What is this precious time which makes no room for love? It is the time of the world. The hands of the clock are the rack upon which love is torn asunder.

Love is not a model of the serious world because the time of love is modeled after eternity. Love is what we are created for and it is what turns our faces toward the living God and his everlasting Kingdom.

The gospel supplies out of itself every possible ground for urgency in the church's mission, because it is the gospel which drives the fundamental questions deep into our hearts. When therefore the church asks these fundamental questions about human existence, it must do so on the basis of an efficacious promise of an ultimate security. Ultimate security is embraced only in our relationship to God. Created for love, we are sustained by the love of him who so created us. We do not see the concrete resolution of the tragic aspects of life and love; but the promise of this resolution has been given, and this promise is here and now efficacious. The church's own life bears witness to the efficacy of this promise.

To persons in bondage to illusions the church proclaims that there is an escape into actuality. That actuality is the everlasting Kingdom that is now. When the church witnesses to this actuality, men catch a vision of a peace which the world neither gives or takes away. But the Now which is the "majestic instancy" of the Kingdom is not to be represented as though it were some ecstatic temporal moment freed from all terminal necessities. Such a projection is a worldly projection; and it is a fraudulent promise made by this world. "Worship me alone and I will give you ultimate fulfillment, an ecstasy without anguish and without surcease"—so runs that fraudulent promise made by the world.

The church's mission in life is not to compound the woes and worries of men but to preach an ultimate fulfillment in divine community. Deeply troubling questions are asked, therefore, in order that people might grasp the actualities of their situation under God. These questions are asked at the Lord's bidding. They are productive questions only when he is the sustaining Presence giving courage to grasp the truth and to love him who is worshiped only in spirit and in truth.

Today we are caught up in a deadly race with time. It is not foreordained that we should run in it until we drop, no nearer the goal than when we were thrust into the race. There is a saving Word for us and for men in all conditions. Let the church bear witness to this Word, and it will be refreshed and become refreshing. Let the gospel be preached, that men may know the Kingdom as it is poised over us, and the Kingdom as it pervades the time of our lives and as it draws us on toward the End. Then we shall have some fair hope of redeeming work from triviality; then we shall be able to enjoy pure play; then we shall be able to love, even as we are loved. Maranatha! Come quickly, Lord!

X

The Living Word in Our Midst

As THE CHURCH GOES OUT INTO THE WORLD TO PREACH the gospel, it is assured of something much greater than all worldly assurances. The Lord of the gospel, the Son of the divine Kingdom, will go with the evangelists, wherever they go. He will be the constant companion in every vicissitude, every disaster, every triumph.

This assurance is for many people in the church little more than a verbal exercise in the air of stale piety. The venerable phrases communicate to them nothing of vivid and potent realities. What we want is something solid upon which to build, perhaps something like an interested or, even better, a captive audience. We need also the sense of having a product sure to go over, once the right angle of approach to the market is figured. We would like a program for which calculable returns are available, to submit to the people who prefer to invest in sure things rather than in risks. Finally, we could use a sound guarantee so that even the people who won't buy will still be friendly and will still find us good Christian people irresistibly lovable.

None of these things is assured the evangelical church. Such guarantees as are given to it are given partly to discipline our natural understanding of success and our natural expectations for success. But this needful work of discipline is only a part of the assurance. The heart of the matter is the promise of the accompanying Presence.

The accompanying Presence reveals all the inviolable freedom of God. God is in no way constrained by our expectations, however keen and hungry they may be. He is not constrained by ecstasies; neither is he necessarily present when ecstasies are the order of the day and night; nor is he bound to make himself known to us when we mouth the words of love. No rite exists to conjure Him.

God is the living Truth who gives himself to the church as the accompanying Presence. Now truth is that by which our spirit grasps what really is. Truth is being mediating itself to the mind and heart of a spiritual creature. By this token the highest degree of truth is that self-representation of being by which at once the ultimate intention of being in relation to ourselves is disclosed, and we are most fully and deeply activated and actualized. When, therefore, the church declares that Jesus Christ is the living Truth, it declares that Christ is the self-representation of God and of the eternal Kingdom. What God is and what God wills for us are made known in Jesus Christ; but these things are made known both from within these actualities and from within our own existence. Jesus Christ speaks from within God and from within man.

The living truth is always with those who bear witness to God in Christ. As the truth, he is also that light which illuminates every man coming into the world. He is with all people, not only with the evangelists. This is hardly ground for jealousy on the church's part. As instrumental to his absolute purpose, he has created in the church a witness to himself. This faithful witness is the basis for everything that the Christian says about the Lord's kingdom; but there is no good reason for supposing that apart from this witness we know nothing about God. There is reason enough to say in the church that we know nothing of decisive importance about the kingdom of God apart from this witness. This witness is the Bible.

The church has the Bible. Whatever is distinctive about the life and message of the church (importantly distinctive, since we must always allow for mere eccentricities) has its roots in this witness. This does not mean that the church preaches the Bible. The church preaches the selfsame Lord and Kingdom to which the Bible points. Hence, if the Bible contains sound teaching, the teaching is a faithful record of goings on of an utterly decisive character. It is not teaching in the sense of sound doctrine. The church cannot avoid having doctrine; but it can hope to avoid putting doctrine in the wrong relationship to concrete actualities and events. When people get so involved with the question of soundness of doctrine, it is always possible that the eventful character of its message will be forgotten or trivialized; in which case the church then becomes a purveyor of world views. And it is then no longer a messenger of the divine Kingdom. It has become at that point a salesman and special advocate for a culture's own evaluation of itself.

When, on the other hand, the scriptural witness is made the effective base of operations, the church can see for itself how dynamic and productive a life it has on its hands. Then it finds itself steeled to face inquisitorial magistrates and all the powers of the world, not in the spirit of bleak defiance, but in hope and love.

The scriptural witness can be made the effective base of the church's operations only under the inspiration of the Holy Spirit, only where this accompanying presence testifies to God and the Kingdom. We know all too well what enormous errors and follies wait to crowd into the church through this very door. What word, uttered either out of solitude or in august assembly, has not been given unholy primacy in human affairs by someone's saying: "It is inspired by the Holy Spirit!" The safeguards against these errors are fragile and vague—we can and we must say, for instance, that the words of the evangelist are fully his—the Lord did not open his mouth and insert them. To say that his words are inspired may mean only that they have been guilded with eloquence or seasoned with wit; or that they prove more edifying in the daily round than one would have supposed. Moreover, words are not the prime effects and signs of the Lord's presence, not even the words of scripture. Concrete life is what he inspires. The holy inspiration is the community of love.

Safeguards such as these seem fragile and vague for several reasons: we set very great store by words; love is so easily counterfeited; we feel that we have lost touch with actuality at so many other points which might serve as touchstones of divine inspiration and as sure signs that the Spirit was with us. Let us look at these matters briefly.

1. We do indeed seem to have unlimited confidence in the power of the word. The man in the street seems to think that if he sees something in print it must be true, or at least nearly true. And we all appear to feel that if we can bombard the world with enough words, we will be able to lead the world up our street, either because it now sees things our way or out of sheer exhaustion. We hope to talk our enemies into their graves. We calculate to sow the seeds of democracy as though the seeds were really rivets to be hammered home with high-powered talk.

2. We can easily see that love is easily counterfeited. Each of us has his own equipment for his purpose. Actions speak louder than words, but not necessarily more clearly; for actions may be designed to lead another into making a commitment advantageous to oneself.

3. We have deep misgivings over the solidity of any rela-

tionship with any actuality that would serve as a firm criterion for the truth of the Word.

If these things are true, we have a great and desperate need for the gospel. The power of that word is not in utterance but in concrete life. The power of that word is the power of real, transcendently righteous and creative love. This alone is the power which can place us in solid and productive relationship to the real world. Hence, while the church has an utterance to make, sermons to preach, hymns to sing, and prayers to offer, above all it has a life to share. Its every proper and seemly utterance concerns this life. This life is God's free sharing of himself in Jesus Christ.

The Christian evangelist is not a salesman for a secular culture presumptively religious at the points at which it is least sure of itself. The Christian preacher is not the salesman of a cult. The gospel messenger is concerned with people as persons; and he does not go among them to pry them out of hell into heaven. He is involved with them because he loves them. Will they be forever lost to the Kingdom if he does not preach the gospel at them and somehow persuade them to accept it as true? This kind of anxiety for others is frequently one's own displaced anxiety for himself. We must pray to be released from this anxiety. Those to whom the church goes are also God's. His will is that now, in this life, in this moment, they should stand, as we should stand, in right relationship to himself. The church does not have the power to determine for others what that relationship is. Its entire energy is to be exhausted in proclaiming the love by which it has been created and which is given for the redemption of the whole creation.

The church is thus an agent for that actual community which underlies all societies and all culture. This community is; it is uncreated, and it is everlasting. And in it all men have their being.

TOWARD A THEOLOGY OF EVANGELISM

When the nature and the power of this actual community are apprehended, revolutions in the spirit and in visible society are certain to occur. And so the church is not deceived when it feels that new social realities may come into existence through the preaching of the kingdom of God. To create these new social realities is not the first task of the church; and their achievement does not complete the task of the church. The demands of the living God run beyond this; and he has revealed through the church a truth which is in no sense the property of the church.

It is not likely that we people of the church will stop worrying about the reception given to us by the world which we are supposed to evangelize. We know, ourselves, how strange the gospel sounds to us, and never more so than when we hear in it a demand for a loyalty above all our other loyalties, and an invitation to a love that will transform our whole existence. And we too feel the pressures, powerful and insistent, upon freedom and integrity. It is not to be wondered at, then, that we of the church should sometimes pressure right back. But in the church we know that this is wrong. The Lord has shown us a more excellent way; and he has promised that if we follow him in this way, he will be with us always.

Out of this assurance a lively family of hopes and expectations is generated. Some of these are fulfilled in this life, and others are not. For one thing, we come around to see that people everywhere need the living word—this is not a freak of culture or of individual disposition. Thereby a great hope is fulfilled—that we should be caught up into an enterprise of transcendent importance and of enduring power. Not everyone will see this; and we cannot hope to have a winning word to say upon all occasions. But when through every reversal and defeat and disappointment we are kept going in the Way, we lay hold of the mighty, living truth in the scriptural witness born by God and to God: "My word shall not return unto me empty."

The unproductive servant, who, confessing his sins, yet clings to grace, is a triumph of Christ. Who will doubt that the church has been again and again such a servant? All glory be to God, Father, Son, and Holy Spirit that it is yet the instrument of his choosing. Amen.

INDEX

Actuality
 34, 43, 50, 53, 56, 105, 109, 110
Americanism
 65, 78
Anxiety
 73, 106, 117
Authoritarianism
 25

Bible
 11, 42, 115

Church
 62, 63-66, 77, 84, 91, 94, 117
Civilization
 68 ff., 71, 78
Commission, evangelical
 9, 11, 20, 24, 40, 56, 62
Communism
 40, 65, 72
Creation
 22, 46, 52

Damnation
 55, 56
Death
 15, 23, 24, 35, 61, 99, 106
Demigods
 15, 79

Democracy
 72, 116
Demons
 30 ff., 59, 61
Despair
 15, 18
Doctrine
 115

Ego
 47, 48, 57, 58
Egoism
 53
Eliot, T. S.
 31
Eschatology
 98-99, 105
Eternity
 37, 105

Finitude
 14, 16, 17, 23, 59
Forgiveness
 32
Freedom
 57, 102, 103, 105

God
 Ch. II, 47, 52, 55, 58, 69, 77, 80, 84, 114

Gospel
24, 40
Guilt
52, 54, 58

History
25, 50, 51, 55, 68
Hitler
19
Holy Spirit
34, 39, Ch. V, 115

Ideals
60, 64
Immanence
16n.
Incarnation
38, 69
Individualism
47, 85
Intuition, ontological
78

Jesus Christ
Ch. III, 56, 60, 96, 97, 105, 114, 117

Kingdom of God
25, 26, 28 ff., 39, 55, 60, 66, Ch. VI, 88, 90, 100, 104, 111

Lincoln
83
Love
28, 38, 46, 49, 54, 61, 88, 89, 109-11, 116

Marcus Aurelius
83

Messiah
30, 32
Metaphysics
24, 36, 38, 44n.
Miracles
30, 35
Morality
17, 28

Nature
35, 43, 44, 46, 47, 49, 68
Norms
49

Obedience
36, 89
Ontology
43

Person
53, 74, 107
Play
106, 108-9
Politics
81, 82
Pontius Pilate
19
Programs, evangelistic
89, 95
Prophet
83, 84

Redemption
23, 56, 57, 76, 77, 100-101
Repentance
29, 32, 86
Resurrection
30, 32-36, 58

INDEX

Revelation
 20-22, 38
Revolution
 Ch. VII
Rome
 19

Salesmanship
 10, 89, 95, 117
Salvation
 76 ff., 86
Sin
 52, 53
Society
 47-48, 50
Solitude
 102n.
Son of God
 36-38

Spirit
 43, 44

Tchaikovsky
 46
Time
 Ch. IX
Transcendence
 16 ff., 18, 20
Truth
 17, 22, 114

Word of God
 9, 38, 88, 89, 96, 97, 114-15
Work
 107, 108

Zebedee, sons of
 28

The Julian Hartt Library
Series Editor: Jonathan R. Wilson

I. *Toward a Theology of Evangelism* (1955).
Introduction by Stanley Hauerwas.

A concise, seminal presentation of the theological vision that Hartt unfolds in his later work. The focus is witness to the gospel, but in Hartt's creative hands that focus illuminates the whole range of reality in compelling ways.

II. *Being Known and Being Revealed* (1957).
Introduction by Walter J. Lane.

A brief, bold proposal for an ontology that reflects Hartt's work on the ontological argument in his doctoral dissertation and his commitment to Austin Farrer's notion of "rational theology" that parallels "revealed theology."

III. *The Lost Image of Man* (1963).
Introduction by John Sykes, Jr.

A theological illumination of significant 20th C. novels and, through them, an examination of the human condition and a proclamation of the gospel.

IV. *Theology and the Church in the University* (1967).
Introduction by Stanley Hauerwas.

Hartt applies his theological powers to questions of commitment and criticism, the role of education in cultural formation and transmission, the formation of identity and morality through education and liturgy, and more. Throughout, Hartt's analysis and exposition takes surprising turns that continue to illuminate the task of theology and the life of the church in the world.

V. *A Christian Critique of American Culture: An Essay in Practical Theology* (1968).
Introduction by David Kelsey.

Hartt's major work defies labels. The subtitle identities it as "practical theology"; by that, Hartt means those doctrines that have immediately to do with the church's mission to proclaim the gospel. Those doctrines are presented in unprecedented ways as Hartt engages in cultural analysis, anticipates much that is found in "missional church" thinking, exposits a Christology and anthropology simultaneously, and sketches a theology of culture that equals any sociology of culture.

VI. *The Restless Quest* (1975).
Introduction by Jonathan R. Wilson.

A collection of essays and addresses that argue for Hartt's understanding of the task of theology of culture (Part I) and the practice of theology of culture as the illumination of our situation (Part II) and our politics (Part III) in the light of Jesus Christ.

VII. *Theological Method and Imagination* (1977).
Introduction by Ray L. Hart.

Hartt applies his wit, insight, and critical acumen to questions ranging across metaphysics, truth, authority, history, imagination and more.

VIII. *What We Make of the World: Memoirs of Julian Hartt (1998-99).*

In these memoirs, Julian Hartt practices the "cosmological theology" that he calls for throughout his scholarly work by reflecting on the everyday, ideal, and natural worlds of his own life. These worlds are shaped by significant times, places, and persons. But most important is the unrelenting honesty of Hartt's narrative as it witnesses to the grace that makes truth and truthfulness possible and bearable in our broken world.

Contributors to The Julian Hartt Library

Ray L. Hart is Dean of the School of Theology and Professor of Religion and Theology at Boston University.

Stanley Hauerwas is Gilbert T. Rowe Professor of Theological Ethics at Duke Divinity School.

David H. Kelsey is Luther Weigle Professor of Theology Emeritus at Yale Divinity School.

Walter J. Lowe is Professor of Systematic Theology at Candler School of Theology, Emory University.

John D. Sykes, Jr., is Professor of English at Wingate University.

Jonathan R. Wilson is Professor of Theology and Ethics at Acadia Divinity College.

www.ingramcontent.com/pod-product-compliance
Lightning Source LLC
Chambersburg PA
CBHW071442160426
43195CB00013B/2006

* 9 7 8 1 5 9 7 5 2 7 8 0 4 *